MOM EGG REVIEW

2015 VOL. 13

Half-Shell Press
New York

Mom Egg Review is an annual collection of poetry, fiction, creative prose, and art by and about mothers and motherhood. *MER* promotes and celebrates the creative force of mother artists and sustains community through publications, performances, workshops, and online at www.momeggreview.com.

www.momeggreview.com
www.facebook.com/themomegg
@themomegg
Contact: themomegg@gmail.com

Front Cover Image: "Reunion" by Tsaurah Litzky. Collage.
Back Cover Image: "Kwan Yin At Rest" by Tsaurah Litzky. Collage.

Cover Design: Sue Altman www.artworksrockland.com

Mom Egg Review is a member of the Council of Literary Magazines and Presses.

This publication has been made possible, in part, by a grants program of the New York State Council on the Arts, a state arts agency, and the Council of Literary Magazines and Presses. *Mom Egg Review* is grateful for this generous support. Mom Egg Review is also grateful for the assistance of The Motherhood Foundation, and for the support of individual donors. With thanks to founding editor Alana Ruben Free and founding publishers, Joy Rose & Mamapalooza.

ISBN-13: 978-0-9915107-0-2   (Half-Shell Press)
ISBN-10: 0991510704

Mom Egg Review
Half-Shell Press
PO Box 9037
Bardonia, NY 10954

CONTENTS

MOM EGG REVIEW
Literature & Art

MOM EGG REVIEW
2015 VOL. 13

Editor in Chief
Marjorie Tesser

Special Poetry Folio
Compassionate ACTION

Guest Editor
Jennifer Jean

Reader
Jennifer Martelli

EDITOR'S NOTE

Welcome to the "lucky thirteenth" annual issue of Mom Egg Review. This collection contains works that reveal truths about motherhood, and about mothers in the world. I know you will find these poems, stories, and art exciting and thought-provoking.

For many, this past year has been an especially challenging one in a string of tough years, a daily toll of atrocities, injustice, and suffering, abroad and at home. Frustration and despair can lead to feelings of powerlessness, resignation, and consequent frozen inaction or unconsidered, precipitate action.

At the center—fittingly, at the heart—of this issue is a special poetry folio focused on the theme of "Compassionate Action". The poems in this section explore and inspire amelioration through action with good will, understanding, kindness, and generosity.

Mothers often have the privilege and responsibility of acting with compassion locally and globally, in interactions with children, the aging and infirm, and the world. This behavior can provide a model and a roadmap to empowerment in urgent circumstances.

Many thanks to Jennifer Jean for curating the Compassionate Action folio, and for Jennifer Martelli for reading for the section. Thanks as well to the remarkable contributors to this issue for their brave, vital works. And I'm continually grateful for the vibrant and growing MER community of writers, artists, and readers, and for your support of this publication.

Warmly,
Marjorie Tesser

Christine Beck

LAST WORDS

At his last, Goethe pled "more light, more light,"
then shuttered up his musings, left the living to consider
what he meant. Some thought he glimpsed the golden
light of afterlife. Others thought it was his epitaph, instructions

for remembrance. Perhaps it was a cosmic joke,
as if he knew he'd spark a scrabbling for enlightenment
among the garrets of undergraduates, desperate
to hitch their slender manuscripts to a star beyond their grasp.

More light, when many die with *mother* on their lips—
the one they had, the one they wished for, the one who lived
next door, her fresh-baked scent that filtered through the window
sash, the broken hinges, gaping undergrowth, the one

who held her body lightly as a loaf of bread, its smooth
outer skin, soft inner yielding, its dailiness as simple
as a dying man, lying in the dark, who wished to feel
once more the daylight streaming in its sustenance.

Elizabeth Lara

IN MY MOTHER'S ATTIC

From her childhood she kept
two thick braids, woven wicks
of gold that lit the lamps
in that dark house.

She kept the starved eyes
of whimpering strays
her brothers brought, their
ragged fur or limping gait.

In a pearl-inlaid box
she kept Euripides, kept
scrims, sets, scaffolds
kept Pandora's last word.

Things she did not keep:
her tiny porcelain tea set;
the seven words in her dream
of the first man she loved.

Olga Abella

IT DOESN'T END HERE

Nothing says thirst like hot air blowing across a dirt field
absent of what was there.

My mother leaves out what she won't let herself remember, three
abortions, a daughter taking pills to die, a sister who set herself
on fire,

the husband who beat the dog almost
to death.

Her skin gathers in clumps at her elbows, under her eyes,
as she tells stories she wants to believe. It doesn't matter if I listen

as I watch the sun twitch shadows
                    across the kitchen floor. Only the words as they sound their way

from the back of her mouth are what I want to remember. Only the voice
                I will want to hear again and again one day.

Her memories, though, are dreams she made up, and if I listen
they will parch my throat with their never becoming.

Sarah J. Den Boer

LETTERS TO LITTLE ONES

my mother conceived me in a hot wind
up in a treehouse with a charcoal floor

the future moved so fast she couldn't cling to
that shoving she felt in her sternum

there were peaches rotting in the corner
I said peaches don't rot

she showed me the identical spoons in the drawer
she hated how they nestled
a small puff of fruit flies escaped

every day, I wore a sundress the color of sugar snap peas
I wanted to eat it from the inside

she said I ate her from the inside
my next move I read in a book

quiet as the inside of an elbow
even a snail can get lost in her own home

there will always be a woman in white and I followed her
or I pretended
my mother didn't want me to be like her
or she did

Rose M. Smith

SURROGATES
a daughter speaks

For truth's sake, Ida, I long still
to tell you I remember
your trapped-doe eyes as Khaki held
me from you, made you target
for his Air Force boots as you cowered,
want to say I was much too young,
a bow-legged spritz of girl
tucked behind his victory snicker,
failing to understand the jagged breach
opened deep within you, but to share these

broken words while you, so frail,
eke your way through long term care,
one hand, one wheelchair revolution at a time,
would be cruelty with no purpose. He's gone
three decades now, a wisp of smoke blowing
over desert spans, a specter on street corners
someplace where they're serving Bud on draft
into friction-clouded old glass steins,
while his goatee, combed, no longer graying,
points back to memories littered
with brash encounters.

I want to tell you which came first—you,
fresh from psychiatric care, frightened
on the stair, or Zola with her strange lilt,
strangled Turkish words, who embraced
him and her daughter lovingly
and fed us—your girls—at arms length
out of pity, thinking what a pair we were,
shuffled into her house from
nowhere else to go but worth the extra rent,
sugar-daddy nights, smoke-filled
rooms saturated with jazz and ready loving.

Time lines distorted by second hands
serve no purpose in your semi-private room,
your endless simply sitting, little left
to say to strangers' faces that surround you

every day. I sit beside you, woman
thinned to skin and bone, and wonder:

Should I say I once hugged Zola, too,
buried my face into her soft below, tried
to find you there, but never called her Mother.
She did not smell the same as you to my five year old
self, and no one can take that homing scent away,
smooth away the imprint long ago ingrained.

Shannon Curtin

THE LEAGUE OF OTHER MOTHERS

By sixth grade I had a list of women
who were not my mother
I could call upon in her absence
if I found myself in need.
A Tupperware coven,
my own list of women warriors,
I imagined them
receiving the call to action
dropping their coffee cups,
and rushing to my rescue.
Aprons like capes,
waving in the wind.

Amy S. O'Hearn

ON DAYS MY MOTHER SMELLED LIKE FISH

On days my mother smelled like fish I curled against
her on the couch while the other six kids

went about the day and into early dusk without her at the stove
or bent before the drier or standing at the line her arms raised

to place the clothes one pin holding two shirts or pants or diaper
in perfect unison for us all. Someone else swept a broom

across the kitchen floor someone carried plates and silver
to the table another folded napkins or poured milk

in mismatched jelly jars and stacked white bread. Someone boiled water
emptied boxes of noodles coordinated the race to our bowls

rang the bell that announced Ready! for father and the boys
who came from behind the paper or in from out of doors

to sit without her at the table though she rarely sat at all.
On days my mother smelled of fish she lay in blue velour

her eyes shaded by an arm, her lips closed her mouth drawn taut.
She let me lie down beside her my body pressed against her womb.

Louie Clay

I DECIDED TO PREPARE MY FAMILY

I told Mother first. It was 1965.

I drove to her hometown, Gadsden,
and took her to Noccalula Falls,
where she and Dad had courted
32 years earlier.

"I need to tell you something
about myself that will disturb you,"
I said.   She looked at me
with loving eyes, in silence.

"I am a homosexual," I said.

She waited a long time to reply.
We could hear each other breathing.
Then she said, "But they have
an operation for that now."

"Not on your life!"
I replied as kindly as I could.

Michelle Robin La

OPEN CLOSED EYES

Flying up in the air, laughing, I leap off my bed onto the toy-covered floor. Crack. Eyes stare out of a split-open head. A baby's face and brown painted-on curls fall away in pieces. It's not even mine. How can I take back a leap? My heart in a knot, I call my mother in to see her broken doll—I've only had it for a few days. She isn't angry, not even sad. Just oh well, things happen. I play with the pieces for a while, round eyes that don't close anymore, before she finally throws it out.

Years later, I'm married and about to have my first child. My mother is remarried and decorating her new home. She shows me a doll's red checkered dress that she's framed in a shadow box. Wide-open eyes in a broken doll head poke out of the corner of my thoughts. Did I break the doll that wore this dress or another? How many did she have? I have pictures from childhood of dolls and animals lined up around me. There are no pictures of my mother with toys. Does she remember my leap? She never said.

Time goes on. My mother visits and my children beg their grandmother for stories about her life. It amuses them that she was a child, the youngest of seven. I overhear a story about a doll she received one Christmas when most of her siblings were too old for toys. "My older sister told me I was spoiled," my mother says. "All she got at that age was a red crayon." My kids laugh with her. It's beyond belief that someone would get only one crayon for Christmas. I've never heard this story before.

After my mother's visit, eyes peek out at me from a doll in a red checkered dress. The gift a youngest child opened at Christmas that represented everything her older siblings never had. Crushed in a moment of play. No need to burden a child. Just oh well, things happen. A leap into my mother's love.

Edward D. Currelley

MY MOTHER'S WAR

I watched my mother navigate the kitchen as if it were a war ship, a destroyer. For her it was entering battle, and nothing less. Her favorite holiday, Thanksgiving. It always brought out the best, sometimes even the worse. Everything had to be perfect, turkey, stuffed and basted, extra stuffing on the side and numerous other dishes prepped and ready to go. We set around silently like little soldiers awaiting her command. When the food was done, the time to dine, hold hands and rejoice in his name everything was complete. We stuffed our faces, laughed, cried and prayed for those who were long gone. My mother smiled, leaned back with an all knowing expression. Knowing there were plenty of leftovers and she did not have to reload to do battle for the next couple of days.

Lorraine Currelley

MAMA

i remember
the taste and love
of mama's food.
awakening to mama in the kitchen
baking biscuits, making grits
and fried fish.
memories of when a stomach full
was a stomach full.

i remember
the sweet smell of mama's sachets,
northern and southern accents
sprinkled with geechee.
regular, good time, neighborhood
church, proud and dignified
women and men.

i remember
mama dancing
skirts and dresses loved her body.
heels created and sung songs
about her strong and shapely legs.
pain, sorrow, loneliness and need
lived buried beneath her smile and laughter.

the joy of children playing.
saturday mornings, radios, cartoons
and chores.
when grace was more than a prayer.
where community cared
and children felt loved and safe.

precious library books,
my little girl poems
unafraid to dream.
taught by family and friends
all things are possible and
God's healing power.

Zachary Bond

AUSCULTATION

Air conditioner dripping in
the parking lot. A new greyblue
dawn: and already hot.

I've got an oscillating fan, her whirled
racket. She makes me feel manic.
I've got a couple

Mannequins in the closet. A few hundred
maquiladoras just beyond
the border. A camera

With a broken focus ring, that might someday
make me whitecake rich, but
which really belongs

In the trash. A pile of chicken skin and
bones, the bigger halves of wishes
ripped in a linoleum, spilled-

Liquor kitchen, where my mother grew up
in sticky vinyl-spine chairs, where
glasses were crushed

During drunken fights between her parents,
the grandpa I never met, my grammy
whose secrets Mom kept from me

Until twelve, when I saw Grammy
drunk or hungover, eyes rung
red, wrinkles like sidewalk

Cracks in her skin, through which
no flowers nor even weeds grew.
Grammy threw up

Her arms that were meant to hold me
that morning, like other mornings
when we played

"Don't Break the Ice," with Law & Order on
in the background. She always saved
her wishbones for me.

She shouldn't have wasted all of them
on me, her meek grandson,
the only one

Of us kids who even remembers her
twelve, maybe fifteen years dead dog
Tammy, who licked my palm

Lapped up the last crumbs from the treat
I'd made her sit for. I can't recall
how small my hands

Were then. No bigger than a minnow,
the only fish I could ever catch.
What a wonder, then—

And what a crime—that each time
in her shadowy glassswept kitchen, she
let me win the wishbone.

When even her dim casket of a future spun
in awful clocky circles. When even, so unfair
though, she should have

Kicked the bottle, picked up her distant middle-aged
daughter and kissed her crumpled forehead,
before she gave away her wishes again.

Heather Haldeman

FIFTY SHADES OF SUNRISE

Six months ago, my eighty-seven-year-old mother was living alone with her long-time housekeeper. Her home, perched on a hill in Bel Air, had fallen into disrepair. Widowed ten years after the passing of her third husband, Mom had become isolated. Her neighbors lived behind gated drives and the narrow, windy roads that led to her house were impossible for her old friends to navigate. My mother -- whom my husband, Hank, claims is a cross between Carol Channing and Phyllis Diller who happens to think she's Marilyn Monroe - had slipped into a solitary world. She used to be the life of the party, a "people person" in every way. Yet, now all her "people" were "on the box" - *Ellen* and *Two and a Half Men*."

I suspected it was her Parkinson's. She'd kept the diagnosis at bay for the past twelve years with medication, but now it was progressing rapidly. For my mother who's all about image, the cane was not enough. And, yet the walker posed a problem.

"I'll look old," she argued.

"You'll look a lot older in a wheelchair after you fall," I told her.

Every time we mentioned Assisted Living, she balked.

"I don't want to be in some room at the end of a dark hallway," she told me. "I want to avoid one of those places like the plague!"

"But, Mom, good facilities are like cruise ships on land," I replied.

Knowing that Mom loves anything having to do with men and prospective romance," I coaxed her: "There are men in Assisted Living."

"I like it here!" she told us. "You're dead if you take me away from what I know."

A fall on her front driveway became the game changer. She'd been rattled, lost her footing with the cane, collapsing like a ragdoll on the hard cement. I couldn't lift her and my friend, Lise, a nurse who lived close by, came to help.

"Well, I dodged a bullet," she said when the MRI showed that she was fine. "Just some bumps and scrapes," the doctor told her. "Beware," he warned, "a fall is what we worry about. Next time you might not be so lucky." That was when she agreed to look at Assisted Living.

My sister, April, and I did research and took her to Sunrise in Santa Monica. On the tour, as if on cue, an elderly male resident driving a snappy blue scooter followed us back to the Director of Sales office.

"Mom, that man on the scooter is interested in you," I told her.

"Really?" she said. Maneuvering her walker in his direction, she dipped her chin slightly and batted her false eyelashes at him.

It wasn't just the allure of the man. The fall had scared her, too. Three weeks later she moved to Sunrise.

Almost immediately upon our arrival, a caregiver whisked her away to lunch. Peeking behind the wall, my sister and I spotted our mother. She was eating alone with the man on the scooter.

"Well, that didn't take long," April, laughed. "And, this one can't leave her!"

"I'm attracted to him, but not physically," Mom told me a week later.

Last Wednesday, on the Sunrise bus ride to a museum excursion, Mom spotted another prospective male. She managed to sit beside him. "Hi, my name is Marilyn…"

"Now, this one," she told me later, "is attractive."

"So, what happened at the museum?" I asked her.

"It was simple," she said. "I told the activities director to position my wheelchair so that he had to get past me to see the exhibit. Worked like a charm."

Meanwhile, she and "The Surgeon" (Mom's name for the fellow on the blue scooter) share pickles at lunch. "He places one on my plate, and I put one on his. It's a thing we do." Yesterday morning, The Surgeon showed up at her door before breakfast, presenting her with a new basket for her walker.

Last night, I sighed when I hung up from a call with Mom. "What is it?" Hank asked.

"She's all in a quandary. Apparently The Surgeon isn't fond of her good friend, Elizabeth. He wants them to eat alone and not have her at the table."

"It's good for your mother to play the field," Hank laughed. "Tell her to go sit with the guy from the bus."

"No, she says that guy eats his meals in his room. But, she's already figured it out. She's not going to let The Surgeon dictate who can sit with at the table."

"That's good," Hank replied, looking down at his smart phone.

"Yep, Mom said: 'All you have to do with a man is throw him a bone once in a while and he's fine.'"

Hank looked up from the phone. "That's not good!" He laughed.

This morning, Mom called bright and early. "Well, it worked."

"What worked, Mom?"

"I sat with The Surgeon last night at dinner. Elizabeth joined us and another lady from Seattle. And guess what?"

"I'm afraid to ask," I said.

"He gave me a wink and put a pickle on my plate."

"See, he's not going anywhere."

"Speaking of that," she said, her tone firm. "If you ever take me out of here, you're dead!"

Dawn Paul

LAST PHOTO WITH MY MOTHER

It's all there: the path through the Audubon Sanctuary,
me standing next to my mother, the light of late afternoon.
It is autumn and the path is full of yellow beech leaves.
We stand close together, her shoulder against my arm,
but we do not hold each other, just the slight leaning in.

How alike we are: neatly built, straight-spined, those long Irish cheeks.
And the genuine smiles. We, who often look hunted in photos,
are happy in golden October, the leaves deep on the path.
We both look directly into the camera, which is held by my beloved.
My mother once said to me, in quiet admiration, "She is so honest.
I can't imagine her ever telling a lie."

If I was as honest, I would say this photo does not tell the entire story.
But another part of me, equally honest, says, once again, it's all there:
the path, the autumn woods, the warmth of her shoulder against my arm.

Jennifer L. Freed

AT THE FAMILY GATHERING

Something in my stomach sours
when she pours out again
my private life, as though
I were still five,
the doings of my days still hers
to offer round the table
with dessert.

I am planning to remind her,
am choosing the right words, balancing
the vinegar with
honey

when I see

her,

nestled on the sofa with my daughter,
child's cheek resting on her
shoulder,
child's small fingers, clasping
hers,

and I
        let go:

Her hands –

        my mother's hands –

so

old.

Janet Barry

PACING

sometimes I wish to walk   as if I am old   and can only manage
a shuffling gait   as if there is an injury to my left hip

this only occurs if I have had a bit too much wine   which
shames me   as I dutifully shuffle about the kitchen feeding the dog

putting away the groceries contemplating the news in which angry people
have done despicable things   or maybe they are desperate people I

don't know   I gimp from table to refrigerator place milk next to cheese
and eggs   the pace seems just right   shuffle - stop - shuffle - stop -

I wonder if it is practice or the real thing   this morning I woke
at 3AM   because the dog wanted to bark at the owls who were intent

on the killing of mice   the procuring of mates   what if all owls were told
forget about it   this quest for food and sex without regard to status   foolish

owls   foolish 3AM dogs   not even getting their hair done their college
degrees their new cars their second houses their retirement portfolios their names

in distinguished journals but this is a ludicrous anthropomorphism which only occurs
if I have had a bit too much shame   the old house going to bits   the old dog

shuffling off to a mud wallow beneath the porch   his left hip placated
with aspirin ground into his dinner and I am placing bread next to butter as I

have always known it should be   laid out on an oak table   a safeguard
against shuffling

Kyle Potvin

BLACKOUT

The nurses wheel you to the TV room
where dark and flooded streets air on the news.

The scenes remind me of New York long ago.
That night you took me to a Broadway show.
At intermission all the lights went dead.
We quickly hushed to let "The King and I"
begin again, to take us back to Siam,
to Anna and Yul Brynner as the King.
But soon we learned the city lost all power.
The ushers sent us off to our hotels.
Unsettled by sirens, shouts, and shattered glass,
we found ourselves alone, six blocks to go.
Steam rose in haunting figures off the streets.
Your fingers gripped my elbow, digging in.
At 12, I'd normally resent this touch
but grasped your hand, afraid you'd lose your hold.

These days your anxious eyes look lost again.
I pull my folding chair up close to you,
about to launch a cheerful monologue.
Yet you surprise me, take my hand and smile
as if we're at that play, still side by side,
believing that the lights will soon come up.

Beverly Butler Faragasso

BATHING

I lower myself into the porcelain rectangle of warm water and I sit facing my mother, our legs intertwined, moist flesh touching. "Who are you?" she demands as she struggles inside my embrace. "Your daughter," I tell her. My mother scrutinizes my face and I wonder if she sees that the color of our hair and skin and eyes is the same and that our flat noses and full lips are almost identical. "My daughter?" she asks. "Yes," I say. "Well," she responds quietly, "you don't look like me." I tilt my head so that I can look directly into her eyes. "I could never be as pretty as you," I tell her, "and that's why you can't see the resemblance." She smiles. "I don't think I have a daughter," she informs me. "Will you let me give you a bath anyway?" I ask her. My mother's face scrunches into a puzzle as she searches my features for the answer: "Do I need a bath?" she inquires. "You have had a long day," I tell her, "a bath will be refreshing." My mother puts her nose in each armpit and sniffs. "I don't smell," she informs me. I hear pride and defiance in her voice – perhaps even a bit of a challenge. "Sometimes," I begin, "we pick up dirt during the day that we cannot see or smell." "So," my mother says, defiance still in her voice, "you think I smell." I do not want to argue and I repeat my original question: "Will you let me give you a bath today?" My mother looks fully at me, her eyebrows arched in surprise. It is a look I saw many times as a child. "What exactly have I been doing all day to get all this dirt on me?" she asks. If she were not in water, each hand would surely be anchored on each hip. I recount all the activities we did earlier, and, when I am finished, I can feel the sag of her flesh next to mine. She closes her eyes and says, "Okay." The warm water has become a little cool and I run fresh, hot water over a washcloth. This new water flows into the tub, warming the old. With the washcloth, I follow the contours of my mother's face, neck, arms, stomach, legs, even between her legs. As I bathe her, I tell her a story I know she does not remember. When my sister and I were little, she often gave us quick baths right before bedtime. They were no-nonsense affairs, because we had school the next day. But, one night, when our mother left us alone for several minutes, my sister and I had a raucous good time blowing bubbles, singing and swimming. Upon returning, arms laden with towels, our mother surprised us by letting her load drop to the floor, leaning over the tub and splashing water in our faces. Suddenly, without warning, beads of water shoot into my face and trickle down my chest. I open and close my eyes. I taste a bit of wet soap. I shake my head and stick out my tongue. I see my mother bring her hands down on the surface of the water with a loud slap. She gets me again. She throws back her head and laughs. I howl with laughter too. Now, it's my turn. I slap the water hard and it flies everywhere – all over her, on the back wall, over the sides, onto the floor, on me too. We laugh and slap water at each other until we are exhausted. We hug. "Mom," I address her in this way for the first time tonight, "do you remember me?" She looks me over carefully in much the same way she did when I first stepped into the bathtub. She then says, "I think someone needs to bathe you."

Wendy Scott

MISSED THE SURGERY

Nine hours of travel
to stand

your arm resting on mine
as you shuffle.

You say, Pull me up.
I say, No. Tuck your feet.

Push yourself up
with your hands.

Like the nurse,
I stand
just out of reach

Alison Stone

FESTIVAL OF LIGHT

Near the table's edge,
my daughter's dreidel wobbles –
a game of chance she can win.

I guide the fire
and tell a fable about miracles.

Last year my mother
lit the menorah, Dad by her side.
She was weak from chemo, and that story
of tenacious flame fed our hope.

Now she's in the hospital, won't let us come.
When I'm home.
Her voice sounds far away.

Her voice sounds far away
when I'm home.
She's still in the hospital; won't let us come.
She's a tenacious flame feeding on hope,
wrecked by chemo. That story.
A lit menorah and Dad by her bedside.

Last year my mother's doctor
told a fable about miracle drugs,
a machine to guide fire.
A game of chance she could win.

My daughter's dreidel wobbles
near the table's edge.

Tsaurah Litzky

ALBA FOR MY GRANDMOTHER

You were stubborn, cunning, fierce as a she-bear with cubs,
no less than death could stop your bustling, your clatter,
your burrowing among the pots for that one small pan to fry
my one small egg, you told me stories, you let me touch you,
you always kept the kettle on, you were rich and yeasty as
your own new bread.

You grew older and older, you forgot my name and called me Ida
after your dead daughter, you told me you didn't want to die, but
they got you anyway and ferreted you away to the land of old people
who wet in their beds. I couldn't stop them, I tried, but not hard
enough and you died alone and cold forty years ago this January.

At the funeral the coffin was closed,
I wanted to read the last note on your face, I wanted to kiss you,
but my Uncle Lepke's wife Clara said at orthodox funerals they
always close the box, as if there could be an end to you, but how
could she know, she was only a daughter-in-law, while I am the
granddaughter of my grandmother, my blessed grandmother
who left to lie down with the worms and tell them stories of
nuptial nights, family fights and morning glories, while they
sing in ecstasy within her like paupers at a holy feast,
I know, I hear them.

Jessie Bacho

WHAT'S DEAD?

My four year-old points to the man on the lemonade carton, *Who's that?* My husband says, *This is Paul Newman. He's dead.* My son, hands sticky with paint asks, *What's dead?* We're waiting for the other to answer. My son pretends to slip on the floor, *Whoa! This is slippery!* Yes. Yes, it is. How do I explain dead to a four year-old? Someday, he'll have to say goodbye to his cats, to his grandparents, to his father, to me. There will be days when he can't eat strawberry jam. He'll save emails for decades to relive conversations with the dead. He'll whisper *I love you* to his sons as they sleep, willing them to stay. The sight of a red bandanna will bring him to his knees. He'll stop eating apple pie after his grandmother dies. He'll avoid the parking lot where he last saw his best friend alive. When my grandfather told me that someday he'd be sky, or when my grandmother made jam and called me *Punkin'* the last time, I wish I'd known that dead means you never get to apologize. You forget the sound of their voice. When someone asks, *If you had a time machine,* or, *If you could have dinner with anyone,* my grandmother passes me the bowl of lima beans because she knows they're my favorite. How can I explain that to him? I watch my husband hand over the lemonade, and my son looks at me for the answer.

Enzo Silon Surin

PREFACE TO EXILE

The last time I saw my mother
before she died wasn't the last.

I was going to come home
that winter, if winter hadn't

birthed in me that conical
tendency to be away—

the vagrancy that had come
and gone during the nights

we'd talk and she'd remind me
that my father's winter had limits,

that I, too, live here.

I had made plans to come home—
if only Chicago had kept its promise,

if only that vagrancy wasn't so
tragically similar to searching for

oneself in the faces of all but the ones
you love. There was no last gaze, no

lurking at the door, like when one knows
goodbye, may preface a definitive exit.

There was no coup to speak of, no last kiss,
nothing that would last passed Thanksgiving,

which later became Christmas, then New Year
and I still had no means of coming home—

but there was always later—before later
became late and the last time, became, was.

John Minczeski

THE DRIFT THAT HER DYING HAD BECOME

Bones washed up on the shore
Of her bed, gasping sea wrack,

Wrack and mire
With not enough oxygen

In all the world,
The room overheating.

She picked up speed
For the final collapse—

Mile markers flashed past,
Winter, the bodies of deer

Lined the side of the road,
The room overheating,

The last of her inner fire
Going cold. The day went cold.

The wind kept up for days.
Ashes up the smoke stack,

Ashes in a plastic box. The snow
Didn't dare stop swirling.

Laura Grace Weldon

FAILURE TOO

Failure is more than shame's
hot tar and feathers.

It's cancer cells
destroyed each day
in the body's
relentless furnace.

The unseen mugger
turning away
as a friend's greeting
crosses the street, bright
streamers through the dark.

The beads of a broken necklace
rolling in his mother's
dresser drawer, evidence
of the long gone afternoon
he scooped blue stones and dust
from the floorboards, crying
until she soothed
with words softer
than her disappointment.

Finding them the week she died
he's glad the necklace broke,
carries those stones
in his pocket to this day,
as ruins remind
us of the splendor
in civilizations that spawned us.

Marjorie Thomsen

SERVING

I was thinking they should cancel night
when I served my saddest
sister her birthday dinner, bowing her

over the plate. Her tears cooled
on my fingertips and soon, melted wax
stuck to the cake.

Prodded by a little madness,
I drew a line in the frosting and licked;
a hardened dot of rainbow blue

entered me. I fail at scouring
the lapis granite top
and taking inventory

of my lapses. But I clean my babies
under their doughy folds, swaddle them
like thick-packaged fish.

It was the season before asparagus
clicked and our men had left us
cold beds. My lips and eyes were tired

from all they had to express
but hands are hands in the nectared kingdom
and flowers test the hoverflies.

Deborah Leipziger

WHAT MY BODY REMEMBERS

I

Throughout the night
The blinds create patterns
On our naked skin
Black and white bands of light
And darkness
Your torso over mine is bathed in chiaroscuro
Our sleep is drenched in bands of sweat and dream

II

My every muscle recalls holding you
My thighs sore from coiling around you
Even now my every movement retains
part of you
My cells retain your finger prints
The way the ocean marks its fish
And the coral ingests sea water

April Clark Honaker

THE WAY SHE CARRIES US

I still keep one photo of us on my bedside table.
In it, we're posing in front of the Fairbanks House
where we stayed on our honeymoon.
His arm is around my waist and I'm leaning into him.
We look happy.
Our daughter carries us around in the mornings
while I get ready for work.
She's always finding new homes for us:
the linen closet, the mouth of my rain boot.
Once she even left us on the lid of the toilet.
I'd like to say I left us out only for her amusement,
but that would be a lie. Our latest home
is the bathroom counter where I stood this morning,
brushing my teeth, as she pushed us into the hole
left by his electric razor. She pointed at us, and said,
"Tell Daddy what you want, Mommy."
I pointed at my foaming mouth, thankful for the excuse,
but she didn't buy it. Jabbing her finger into his chest,
she said, "Look. Daddy's right here.
Tell him what you want." By this time, I was spitting,
thinking, It doesn't matter what I want, what you want.
He'll never be able to give it.
Instead, I rinsed out my mouth and said, "I want Daddy
to get better, and I want him to love you.
I want him to spend time with you."
Then it was her turn. "What do you want?" I said.
"Tell him what you want." She looked away, dragged us
off the counter, and sulked around the room,
swinging us from side to side at least seven times
before landing us back on the counter.
Then she looked at him through eyes just like his
and said, "Daddy, I want to go there."

Lisa Vihos

SELLING MY SON'S BUNK BED AFTER THE DIVORCE

You could tell that I was on the verge of tears
as you and your husband loaded the skeletal parts

of the knocked-down, maple wood bunk bed
into the back of your pick-up truck. You said,

It's in really good shape and I said,
It was a good bed. That's when you heard

my voice crack, and mother-to-mother,
you knew how I felt. You said,

I know I will feel it when I take the crib down.
I said *yes, it's hard to do these things,* and I turned

so you wouldn't see my eyes. We had already
exchanged glances, you and I, when your husband

snapped at you about the large container of dirt
he had not removed from truck before coming over.

I wondered how it was for you and your daughters,
living with such a short fuse in the house. You and I

shared the same first name, but more, we relished
the child's bed; a place where the future dreams itself.

I left the four of you and turned into my new house.
Minutes later, I heard doors slam, little girls cry.

I didn't want to look. I only wanted the bed
to go forth firm, so we could all, at last, be happy.

Francine Rockey

SKY

The broken
coffee mug misses you.
The rinsed dish in the sink,
the right side of
                the couch
and the left side
of the bed
miss you. I lock the door of the house
        that misses you and walk
slow through the stinging sun
            children skipping
rope in the park sing:
Teddy Bear, Teddy Bear, turn out the lights.
(I think of missing you).
There's an old man on the swings.
Dressed like he's just learned
to choose his own clothes:
an argyle vest and a light blue baseball cap.
I sit on the swing beside him.
His smile
knows something of missing.
        I fling my toes to the clouds
dip my head toward the earth
        till I'm curved like the arc of the sky
(The sky that misses you).

DUET

The slight curve of my belly reminds me
I didn't make you up. The rings around my eyes

haven't faded yet. Gurgles within caverns
of my stomach echo louder, food not satisfying

the hollowness. The only easy part
was naming you—Jacob, have I loved.

Now you are star stuff. A doily-sized blanket.
Tiny blue cap. Soft stamp of your footprint.

I was never stronger, or weaker, than in the moment
of hello-goodbye. No screaming, no clamor.

No cause, no whimper. Just a fading,
as night became day again.

Quinn White

TUMBLING

Cells followed their zygotic path.
This was no war zone.

I decorated a tree with paper snowflakes.
I unwrapped a ruby necklace, tickets to a sunny place,
lipstick made of crushed diamonds, a mink teddy bear.
I pulled green strings and bows deflated.

That year no one taped my boxes.

A fork, a plate, a piece of pecan pie was a vignette
framed by a lace napkin I could stain if I chose.

A court date came. I signed papers.

On the way home, an engraved crocodile wallet,
caviar and crackers, someone pointed to a chandelier,
said "Yours if you want it." I did and rode to Applegate Lane,
copilot to the sound of crystals. Teardrops trapped

and released light until the car was a raw gem tumbler.

I napped while a visitor dismantled the tree.

My name was cursive silk on my nightgown.
A hospital date came. A nurse pointed to a baby,

"Say goodbye." I did and cards arrived.

Thinking of me. Embossed with angels
who surveyed and assured us all

a plan existed and we followed that plan.

Darcy Smith

EGG SHELLS

2 am soaked in sweat.
Weight of my hair flames the back of my neck
I clutch my tanned and tired thighs
the quivering refuses to stop.

Institution green walls rise with swells of labor
A sea of unrelenting pain plummets down
my breath my anchor.
He he who. He he who. He he whooo.

My labor coach's sad strong blue eyes pierce past pain.
We breathe in absolute unison, braiding bravery from fear.

Another contraction crashes down, knocks me to my knees
Labor, a prize fighter, sends me back to my corner of the ring.
My husband hovers with a glass of juice and a smile filled with hope
I wave him away like a fly on food
Breathe with me or get out.
He he who. He he who. He he whoooo.

An anesthesiologist enters.
"Just breathe normally." he insists,
waving a mask near my mouth.

I'm groggy, a little loopy and have no idea why.
I hear nurses murmuring
"Someone has to tell the mother."

I slip into dreams of my Nana.
Salt of the earth, eyes steely grey green
She sifts flour, blanketing the entire kitchen table as the
sun peeks through a powdery waterfall
She builds a center well then pulls an egg from the front pocket of her faded floral apron.
Yolk dives in slippery.

Cracked shells linger,
empty and open.

From my bed, I hear voices again, this time I'm sure it's my mother.
A petite woman with black bear like loyalty, awakened from her slumber

Her family threatened, she roars in the hallway.
Tears open my doctor's grief stricken heart
"What the hell were you thinking?"
I slip back to sleep.
Nana stands quietly working the flour,
coaxing shape where there was none.

I wake to a nurse's steps, heavy and sullen.
Her gaze downcast, her cheeks ruddy and swollen.

I beg with my eyes.

She shakes her head. Holds my hand.
We cry together. And don't say a word.

My husband takes slow tender steps towards me
cradling our son who is swaddled, silent and perfectly still.
His lips full and pink, dabbed at the edges with blue.

The nurse pulls a hospital bed next to mine.
My husband's long arm reaches across an abyss of linoleum,
We lie side by side, fingers cradling tears as we slip into sleep and our
Hands hang
empty and open

Emma Bolden

AFTER YOUR HYSTERECTOMY: WHAT CAN YOU EXPECT?

The nurse's first question is difficult: "Age," she says, inflected at the end to indicate the interrogative mood. You sit for a minute. You say, "Thirty-four." You feel like you are lying. You feel as confused as you feel in the Rite-Aid's vitamin aisle, standing and wondering, *If my body is technically over fifty but chronologically only thirty-four, do I take Centrum Silver or Centrum Daily?*

The nurse's second question is also difficult. She asks, "Is there a chance that you could be pregnant?" You say, "I had a hysterectomy when I was thirty-three." She says, "Oh, were you finished having children?" You say, "I don't have any children." She says, "Are you married?" You say, "No." She doesn't ask any more questions. You sit with her in the small sterile room, listening to the blood pressure monitor's cuff inhaling, exhaling, and inhaling again.

You and your bladder are experiencing a breakdown in communications. Your bladder does what it wants and when it wants and it refuses to warn you. It also refuses to explain. So does your doctor, who shrugs and says, "It happens." And it keeps happening: when you sneeze and when you cough, and when you laugh so hard you snort, and when you scream at the person who stole your parking space, and every time you forget to wear a sanitary pad.

You threw out all of your sanitary pads the day your surgeon released you from his care. You re-bought as many sanitary pads a few days later. You feel guilty about wasting all of that plastic and money. You feel guilty about yelling at the person who stole your parking spot.

You can't sleep. You can only sleep. You wake, in the indigo of the hours past midnight, to sheets sweat-soaked until sopping wet.

Your fingertips are always wrinkled, as if you've spent a year suspended in pool water, holding your breath, looking upward and into a blue you think you remember as sky. You break at least one fingernail a day. They splinter and splice, down to the quick.

You fall while walking up your front steps and worry about small breaks, parting the surface of your tibia like strands of hair. You install a handrail and motion-sensor lights. You wear sturdy shoes, even indoors. You take calcium, daily, dutifully. You take estrogen and progesterone. You take bags of frozen peas and press them to the back of your neck, just like your mother did when she was struck with hot flashes.

Your hair, which once twisted and tangled in curls down your back, now hangs flat, sheet-straight. Every time you shampoo, it falls out by the handful.

Your mother tells you that her best friend's daughter is pregnant, and you hear the hairline fracture in her voice. You hear the same fracture in your voice when you say, "Oh, that's wonderful. Tell her I said congratulations."

You start wearing caftans because it seems appropriate.

You will never find a book titled *What to Expect When It's Totally Impossible for You to Be Expecting.*

You stand in a crowded living room, wearing a caftan and a sanitary napkin and a gin buzz, and someone asks you a question. You rub your chin, which is what you do when you want someone to know you are considering a question and very carefully. Then you feel them: hairs. Terrifying, hard little wiry hairs. You spend the rest of the night with your face angled away from everyone you talk to, or with your hand on your chin. You hope everyone is thinking *she is such a good listener* and not *look at those hard little wiry hairs on her chin.* At home, you run towards the bathroom and the magnifying mirror, towards the tweezers stationed permanently next to it.

You find six hairs on your chin.

The next day, you find four hairs on your chest, sprouting from the skin that covers your heart.

You stand by the Rite Aid's Mother's Day card display, confused. Every card says that you hope you're a good mother, just like your mother taught you to be. You search for any card that doesn't say you are a mother. You say to yourself, *there has to be one. There has to be just one.*

You never find one. Not even just one.

Even though you live alone, you only cry in the shower. You don't plan it that way: the shower is always, simply, the place where it hits you, whatever it is, harder and hotter than the hard water hitting your back. You find yourself crouched in the tub with your knees to your chest. You slobber and scream. You cannot make words. And then you stand up. You scrub shampoo into your hair. You rub the handfuls of hair that fall out between your hands, sticking it to the shower wall so you won't forget to throw it away, just like your mother taught you. You dutifully apply conditioner. You dutifully gather and throw away every last straying strand of your hair.

Jane Harrington

THE WAITING ROOM

Sami, a young woman on "Days of Our Lives", is filled with a great deal of anxiety because of a terrible secret she possesses, one that she worries will drive away a man she is soon to marry. There is something in her oblique references to the concealment that hints at sordidness, keeping all eyes in this room riveted on the flat screen. A raspy-voiced older woman is counseling her now: "Tell him before he finds out from someone else." Dramatic pause. Close-up of Sami's trembling lower lip. A pluck of harp strings, and the scene shifts to an-other couple of people having another snippet of conversation about a problem that, like Sami's, won't find a resolution in this hour.

Long louvers clank against the windows with each surge of conditioned air from the rattling box beneath, letting in only the occasional slivers of natural light, which prick the cushions of vinyl chairs and the pointed leaves of nandinas so obviously synthetic that the usual urge to feel the plant, to *know,* is entirely suppressed. A tattered *Cosmo* lies on the table in front of me, its near-naked cover model smirking at the ceiling, promising to reveal sex tricks to anyone who flips the pages. Tiny spots wrinkled into shiny paper give the appear-ance that a raincloud has lingered over it before moving on to the rest of the fare—*People, In-Touch, Style.*

I look to the receptionist again, who is taking another clipboard from another teenage girl wearing the same sullen expression Mel wears, the same too-long sleeves. Surely, I keep thinking, this woman will have an awakening, will shoot out of her seat, sweep all these magazines away and replace them with a catalog from the National Gallery of Art, a report on the progress of women's rights in India, the latest magazine from the Nature Conservan-cy, anything. And then turn on the travel channel so the cutters and mothers of cutters can escape from this room.

Perhaps the psychiatrist's actual office is better. Maybe there are no magazines, no television to distract as the doctor encourages Mel to talk about her problems. Have they, I wonder, gotten to the part about a mother's/my failings? How it took months before a mother/I noticed that her duvet was blood-stained, realized her trash bin was filled with the same evidence on tissues, actually read some of the tiny scraps of paper she had been dropping around the house like molted feathers—those obsessive scratchings of calorie counts as she picked herself to nothing in front of her mother's/my eyes?

"I don't know what I'll do if I find out I'm pregnant!" a desperate teenager screams from the wall, advertising a local hotline.

I don't have to watch this, I tell myself, setting my eyes on the floor, on my cold feet in sandals, on my lap. And there it is—a ladybug. I don't know if it landed there from flight or crawled up the leg of my jeans. In any case, it is not moving now. I nudge it, but it re-mains inert. It is an orangey color, a faded version of the deep red ladybugs I see in my own garden at home. They like to eat the aphids set on destroying the milkweeds I plant to feed the monarch butterflies and their larvae on their periodic visits to my yard. The aphids have been a scourge this summer, too many for the ladybugs to keep up with, so I, too, had started picking them off, watching each day for new clusters. But now I just watch Mel, as if we're standing together on a high pier. If I look away for just a moment, she could chase a gull, be gone.

She's out here now, swollen-eyed and mascara-smudged, standing at the laminate counter and making a new appointment with the receptionist, whose glance keeps darting to the television. Sami has just appeared on someone's porch and is ringing the bell. A nurse is calling out the name of one of the other teenage girls, who is moving unhurriedly, distractedly, obviously hoping to first find out who it is that Sami seeks there. Her betrothed? Is she going to confess? But the hour is up; the harp strings join a full orchestra; the credits rush by; a breathy voice imparts its wisdom: "Like the sand of time moving through the hourglass, so are the days of our lives."

I look down at the ladybug, still there on my jeans, still still. And then, just as I lift a hand to swat it away, it starts walking, slowly, as if waking from an unconscious state. I look up at the faux nandinas, and then I pick up the little insect, close my hand around it, and wait by the door.

Libby Maxey

UNDERSTANDING

I said I understood, and it was true
As far as narrow understanding goes.
A sightless leech and small, it only knows
The compass of its mouth, the feel of you
Just there, just then, the spot of skin it drew,
The bit of blood it raised before it fell
Away, the mouth still gaping—not to tell,
But straining to take hold again. Too few
The days when it might find you waiting, still,
The water past your waist, exposed but for
The modesty of shadows—now restore
That slim yet certain seal, and now refill
The guessing space with present verity
To reassure me that I almost see.

Sarah Shamel

PANTOUM FOR THE BOYS AT Q'S PARTY

"And many years more!" we wish at song's end
For my freckled birthday boy and his friends.
But the lads don't linger on wishes of parents.
To the graveyard to hang the piñata!

For my freckled birthday boy and his friends,
Nature beckons on this first day of spring
To the graveyard to hang the piñata,
Above bodies that fell long ago.

Nature beckons on this first day of spring.
Hear the bat crack - boom! - and then rain,
Above bodies that fell long ago,
Scatter treasures, boys gather the pieces.

Hear a bomb crack - boom! - and then rain.
Last sound heard by soldiers beneath us,
Scattered treasures, grown-boys blown to pieces,
Dispersed 'cross freshly-damp soil.

Last sound heard by soldiers beneath us,
Boys heeding their thirst for adventure.
Dispersed, 'cross freshly-damp soil,
The children collect flags from graves.

Boys heeding their thirst for adventure,
Oblivious to the honor of soldiers
The children collect flags from graves
Like this territory is theirs to plunder.

Oblivious to the suffering of soldiers,
Will these boys become men who wave weapons?
Like this territory is theirs to plunder:
World caught in a cycle of war.

Will these boys become men who wave weapons?
Not lingering on wishes of parents:
That the world break this cycle of war.
That our boys have many years more.

Margaret Rapp

REFLECTIONS OF A MULTICULTURAL MOM

On my son's third birthday, he got chicken pox. We cancelled his party, but I still gave him the present he most wanted—a Barbie doll. Although I am a "modern" Mom, I was a little uncomfortable giving him a Barbie, so I gave him a Barbie and Ken; and, since he is an inter-racial child and I wanted to be politically correct, I gave him a black Barbie and Ken (although Barbie did have a blonde streak in her hair). My son loved his gift and I can still see him, sitting in front of his cake with a birthday hat on, his face speckled with pox marks, holding up his Barbie (Ken had already been relegated to the unused toy box).

For the next two weeks, while he was recuperating, Barbie was his constant companion. When he went back to daycare, he wanted to take his Barbie for show and tell. While I had my misgivings on how the other children would react—would they make fun of him—I stuck to my feminist principles and didn't discourage him. That afternoon when he came home, he threw his Barbie angrily in the corner. My first thought was that he had been teased or called a sissy. Then he tearfully said the words that are still imprinted in my mind. "I want a white Barbie." He had never used the word white to refer to a person before. Years later, I learned that it was actually Jessie, a black girl who lived down the block, that had taunted him about his "black" Barbie.

I hate the word "bi". Like in I am the mother of a biracial child. I keep expecting to see a child that is painted black on one side and white on the other like those mimes you see in the park standing like statues. It comes from that puritanical Calvinism where everything in America is bifurcated, cut in half, polarized. Like either/or, good/evil, black/white. And you are always expected to come down on one side or the other.

Murphy Brown was very big on TV when my son was small. After his Dad took off, I played the Murphy Brown role—the fast talking, independent woman who raised a child on her own. It worked very well until they found out I had a mixed race child. Even then, it could work if they thought he was adopted. Once they found out I had him the old fashioned way, I was relegated to the welfare Mom role—the woman who was too stupid to keep her legs together and was dumped when she got pregnant.

I know that my son has spent much of his childhood longing for some traditional nuclear family that he will never have (as do many children from both black and white homes). But our society is much more multicultural now than it was when my son was born twenty-six years ago. These days he self identifies as a German Haitian Dominican Jew. And we do have a "biracial" President.

My son is grown now—a muscled young man with light golden skin, deep dark eyes and the somewhat rounded features that compliment his dimpled smile. His dark curly hair is slowly turning into male patterned baldness—a trait which I find attractive but I suspect he is embarrassed by as he has taken to wearing a hat. He lives with a friend in Harlem and writes lyrics for a pop singer that plays the small downtown clubs. Like most starving artists, he walks dogs to pay the rent, It is hard to believe that he is actually a grown man who has to lean down to hug me instead of looking up at me. So why am I still so worried?

Sunday afternoon a couple of years ago, my son called me from the police station. He was picked up at 6am in Harlem in front of his house. When he protested that he had rights, he was arrested. After two days he was released. He spent two days in jail, lost two days work for which he was not paid, his only good winter jacket was torn when he was roughed up and he saw a homeless man beaten down by police while he was in the holding cell.

The particulars of why he was arrested aren't important. The charges were dropped, the judge apologized. His legal aid attorney told him he should file charges for false arrest. He made some halfhearted noises about filing charges, but never followed through. He seemed defeated by the whole experience. When I told people what happened, indignant at my son's mistreatment, the first question they asked was what did he do wrong? After a while, I kept quiet about it, ashamed that he had been arrested. I began to believe he had done something wrong. And I wondered if he would have been arrested if he had been white.

Two months ago he told me he was frisked again in the same neighborhood on his way to work. This time, when the arresting officer "copped an attitude" when he tried to find out the reason he was stopped, he didn't say anything and let her frisk him because he didn't want to be late for work. I didn't know if I was more relieved that he had chosen the pragmatic approach to stay out of jail or saddened that he had learned the lesson society expected him to learn—that he is a second class citizen who knows enough to shut-up and keep his head down. And he was still late for work.

Recently my son told me he was glad that he had been raised in an "alternative" family. He felt that it gave him a more worldly and tolerant outlook on life. What I learned is what it feels like to worry every time my son walks out the door.

Margie Shaheed

CATCHING THE BUS #6

2:45 PM Irvington, NJ 07111

Music hammers its way out of the open windows of a pimped-out gold metallic 1976 Impala parked right in the bus lane, rising and falling, loud and sharp, against the afternoon's blazing sun. A reddish-brown Aunt Jemima Cornbread-colored woman dressed like an unmade bed stands posed in a heroin nod.   The haze engulfing her short frame props her body up at the knees which keeps her from falling.   The center of her right palm and fingers, dangling from her side, are smeared with the sugary glaze of a half eaten Honey Bun crumbling in her hand. I watch her openly as I wait for the bus to arrive, without shame, and I wonder what would make her want to stop the world and step off? Is it life's piss stains?   And, I wonder, how will she find her way back to us? Will she leave a trail of crumbs?

The bus driver swoops down on us swiftly. Nudged by an invisible hand, the woman pulls herself up as an accordion, boards the bus, pays her fare with difficulty, and heads straight to the back where she takes a seat among a snickering chorus of school children packed like peanuts in a jar. I realize there's a faint feeling inside of me that says somehow I need to protect her. I follow her haze to the back of the bus amazed at how she navigates through the wreckage. I feel lucky to find a seat across from her so that I can continue to watch. Through narrowing slits, the woman looks around at the kids for a few seconds, and then runs her tongue over the nubs of missing teeth and gums, hydrating the desert stuck on her lips. She scratches away the itch nagging both arms, and as if on cue she proceeds to nod. The children know the woman is high and vulnerable and all their attention turns towards her. The amusement and mischief of children pushes them to the brink, they point fingers, stare the woman down, whisper and giggle in each other's ear, talking low as if they've just shared their first dirty joke.

The oldest boy stands up a few feet facing the woman, looks at her dead center, lifts his leg, and stomps his foot on the floor of the bus as hard as he can.   The thunder and clap of the sudden noise lifts the woman up from her pit. Laughter is a contagious virus running rampant. The boy has moved quickly back to his seat snatching his head so that he looks away from the woman, as does the others sitting nearby, even though they continue to watch her peripherally as they laugh their asses off. The woman's eyes, wide and confused, flip-flop and shuffle from person to person trying to locate the source of the boom, oblivious to the fact that she is the butt of a silly joke. Not finding the noise, the woman gives up, closes her eyes, slides into a heroin lean, and nestles back in the quiet of her ditch. The boy stands up again. I know what he's about to do so I look up at him directly with a facial expression that says, "you had better not!" He tosses my stare aside and stomps his foot louder than the first time. The woman is shaken loose again. This time I don't ask the boy to stop, I tell him to stop like I imagine his own mother would do. He's so tickled by the woman's confusion he can barely pull the word, Ok out of his mouth, but he manages to and slyly returns to his seat.

By now, the woman begins to realize what's really going on and she's pissed off. The bus driver calls out over the speaker, "Halsey Street." The woman gathers herself and spits curse words at the children's feet as she prepares to leave. They respond by calling her a dope head, a crack head, a bitch. This time I admonish the whole group and remind them they would not act like this if their mothers were here. They agree by looking down and the heckling stops. We all watch the woman intently; our eyes burrow holes in her back, as she leaves the bus disheveled with a string of babbling obscenities trailing her out of the door.

Nancy Lynée Woo

KARMIC JUSTICE

Many of us write to set things straight. When records are bullied by the person in charge, the underdog publishes a pamphlet. My dad says Chi-sing would hate for her bastard grandchild to be writing about her. She is the center to which all stories spin. Her father, Gung-gung, was a very rich man before the war. She was Daughter #1. More like a man, my dad says of her. The one in charge. Psychic. No one contradicted her. She could stare you down for years. Once, she thought her sister cheated her at mah-jongg so she didn't speak to her for a decade. Wonderful family, she said of her kin. Best son, she said of her brood. Tall. Handsome. Smart. Doctors. Going to marry Chinese. You want to see fireworks? Try bringing her white ghost granddaughters to the house for Christmas. She'd storm out screaming. My psychic tells me the man I love who will never love me back was probably my son in another life. What did I do to him? My conscience screams at me to surrender. I feel lucky to know at least what debts I'm paying. In this life, he will never love me. He will never be able to love me. For a while, the Chi-sing inside of me wants to strangle any other idea than the one I prize. Throwing karma can be heavy. I make it my job to let go. It's a challenge to give love. A puzzle to forgive. When I feel the dark sink into me, I let it tremble. I let it plunge. I riproar all the hate-energy around and out. Out. You want to talk about pure? You've got to talk about cleansing. When things get dirty, I scrub. I scrub the spaces around the third eye, for that's where my daughter will be born.

Donna Katzin

SURVIVORS

Along the road to Chokwé
potholes devour axels,
ant hills that have rebuilt themselves
from nowhere after the floods
vie with women, bags and buckets on their heads
Plastic sacks of cashews cling
to the trees.
Where the waters have receded
Maria plants again.
Of her ten children,
four who lived remain
to be fed.
It will be months until the harvest.
When she finishes her hectare,
she helps Fernanda, belly in bloom,
who scratches soil crusting in the sun.
Her hoe aches in her hands.
She teaches with her fingers, feet, spine—
stay strong,
leave no one alone.

In Southern Mozambique, the Limpopo River flooded in 2013, leaving devastated communities.

Meredith Trede

TAKING BACK THE DAUGHTER OF THE NIGHT

Nemesis, daughter of the night, mark
    this phase of turning year. Make autumn's
        equinox expanding dark the perfect time to set

the world to rights. They say you used to share
    the luck, dish out the righteous anger of the gods,
        your special prey those grown too rich, too proud.

We beseech you, Nemesis, daemon
    of divine wrath, partisan of retribution,
        we need you now: pay back the counterfeit

pious; the bloated stockpiling plunder;
    they who blindly bid our soldiers shoot; let
        their deeds seal their fate. Bestow your genius.

Tsaurah Litzky, "Kwan Yin At Rest"

Compassionate ACTION

A Poetry Folio

Jennifer Jean, Editor
      Jennifer Martelli, Reader

ON THE "COMPASSIONATE ACTION" THEME

by Jennifer Jean

Compassion is action. So, why "Compassionate Action"? When I chose the theme with Mom Egg Review editor Marjorie Tesser, I liked the thought of a theme articulated by a double-positive. I'm sick of a world in the minus! Also, I'm sure I'm not the only one who gets muddled about the difference between compassion and empathy (which is sharing or vicariously feeling another person's suffering); and, between compassion and sympathy (which is a remote feeling, merely one's own mustered-up sadness for another's suffering). My friend Laurette Folk, a novelist and the editor of *The Compassion Project: an Anthology*, says, "To cultivate compassion we must first define it for ourselves." Compassion is action. It is shared feeling with another person's suffering, coupled with a desire to alleviate that suffering. Sometimes we can alleviate suffering. Too often we can't. Moms in particular understand this. However, the authentic desire to make a difference is real movement in the world. It's a push forward through pain. A body at rest tends to stay at rest; a body in motion tends to stay in motion; so, compassion, which is movement, gets us all to a new place. To change. Writing is also action. I wrestled for a while with this truth when I started writing my second poetry manuscript about human-trafficking and objectification in America; I kept thinking, "Does a poem about the commercial/sexual-exploitation of boys (for instance) really do anything, change anything?" But writing causes unseen ripples—people are reached with information, are moved by beauty (if I can write well enough!). Folks are moved, by the vulnerability and authenticity they encounter, to write about issues closest to their hearts. (I've seen this happen in reaction to some of my poems on human-trafficking.) We had so many wonderful pieces submitted for this folio and each writer rippled the world with their words of hope, longing, anguish, ferocity, indignation, love, and compassion. I want to express my thanks to everyone who trusted us with their work; and thanks also to Marjorie, and to *Mom Egg Review* Reader Jennifer Martelli.

Nina Rubinstein Alonso

IF THAT WAS HER NAME: TANGIER

1.

Silver green melons like piled up
moons—trays of sun struck pastry
copper brass leather perfume

the medina's dark and narrow
needles of light pierce clots of shadow
embroidered djellabahs and amber beads

charming until a boy dashes by
yanking down on my left hand
trying to grab my gold ring

failed baby thief runs so fast
glancing back to see what I'll do—
tighten my fist and keep walking.

2.

Men offer themselves as guides
or anything else we'd like

kif bhang sex hashish
what's easiest is nod and smile

repeat brief courteous lies
not now thanks maybe tomorrow

until they give up
a veiled woman squats

by a mound of dusty carrots
her wrists circled by red sores.

3.

Pyramids of perfect golden pears
but the vendor shakes his head
no English no French no Spanish

until a woman in a gray hijab
translates Arabic for us
then points toward

the highest plaza in Tangier
leading through twisted
alleys up stone steps to see

ships suspended on the world of water
Spain the distant gray blue of clouds
leaning close she says

"I'm Fatimah—the last two years
my husband's in France
sends little money

I'm a nurse with three small children
he won't return or agree to divorce
even though he's abandoned me

married women have
no rights--no passport
unless the husband signs."

4.

She pauses then adds
"Meet me tomorrow noon"
and slips down the stairs

Fernando shakes his head
"What can we do for her
even at the embassy?

it's going to be about
money"— but next day
we come back carrying
a bag of figs

dark honey brushed
by butterflies as we have
nothing else to give.

5.

Veils on women's faces
veils wide as centuries
I see black husks

with voiceless women inside
mute bags of cloth
curled around fear

forget theory and philosophy
in this marketplace at this time
to pull off a veil could cost your arm.

6.

An hour waiting — no Fatimah—
Fernando checks his watch while

a boy tries to sell me cheap bracelets
keeps pushing them at my arm

another half hour—no Fatimah
if that even was her name

yesterday she opened her shell
but one pinch of fear collapses the heart

Fatimah takes no second chance
veils close every woman we see.

7.

Back in the hotel garden green
parrots stretch chained wings
a turtle dozes under our table

I'm not much for cards
but recognize a losing hand
we had no idea how to play

hours waiting for Fatimah
or whatever her name might be
but what else could we do

for a few minutes our shadow
touched hers and the best
I can do is tell you.

Rethabile Masilo

THE MOTHER

The woman's hand reaches
around her child and brings the shawl
full circle, to pull the fabric tauter
against drops of rain
on those dreadlocks that some
have told her to get undone,
or cut, or else accept never to work
in this town again. Except, how
do you disentangle a story from itself,
and where does one even begin?
She thinks of her Rasta man,
who months ago fled into the arms
of another woman. There is work
to be found, cherished and kept
if the street is ever to be left,
her child sent back to school,
if there is ever to be anything
in the world beyond this, there are things
to plan for and do, a way to remove
the tattoo on the small of her back
and frame an image of it in her life,
a new man to love who will take both
of them by the roots of their dreadlocked
heads and plant them in the middle
of his life, and water them a little.

Megan Merchant

GAZAL FOR UNSPOKEN SORROW

What will become of us, our son resting along the line of my hip, hum.
The sweet whimper-whine his breath makes, lip pressing lip, hum.

In our half-dark, we hush hands and mouths while he's asleep in the room,
the stretched and scarred afterbirth of my body unfolding a deep rooted hum.

Thin white milk streams from my nipples onto your chest, a praise of unspoken sorrow.
My body weeps without permission, a primitive, broken *hum*.

A Monk said, you cannot know compassion until you love your own mother, absolutely.
If I exhaled completely, I could die from such abandon, my heart shutter-stopping hum.

Today, I light three candles, chant, *Om Mani Padme Hum.*
Megan, let compassion have the gravity of stone. *Om Mani Padme Hum.*

Laura Foley

TRANSFERENCE

The inmate says he wants
to smash someone's head
against a concrete floor.

*My brother's stolen
my land, and here I am
stuck in jail.*

His face is livid,
his fist twitching.
We spend all day

meditating in silence;
eight hours in a quiet room
with a concrete floor,

I breathe his anger in.
The next morning,
my neck's so stiff and sore,

I have to hold my head
with my hands to save my neck
from its weight.

The inmate punches a guard,
is strait-jacketed,
taken upstate.

Six months till my head
and neck exhale, six months
to heal the ache.

Megan Merchant

KNEEL

"I am certain that the Lord, who notes the fall of a sparrow,
looks with compassion upon those who have been called
upon to part, even temporarily, from their precious children."
                                    Thomas S. Monson

here at the threshold of war.
Wet your lips, smooth
the grime from your blistered feet.
No more walking,
this is home enough now, the moon
will be out soon
and ready to plug the bullet holes
in the sky with stars.
If it's worth praying, I will pray with you
in the language of olives.
We'll kneel on the grove floor, press
our lips to the chalky soil
and tend to love. Our breath will ink
the invisible names
of the dead onto the dampened leaves,
and when the sun
breaks the morning wide, the wind will dry
and carry them home. Follow.
There, you will be greeted by mothers and wives
and allowed to weep
against their breasts until your words smooth
into the tea kettle whistle.
Do not worry if the cups are cracked, they'll
still hold. Drink with honey and have
patience with the bitterness of grief.
It will try to tear
the thin fleshed fruit, rush the feast.
Wait for it to rot
and open, for a single seed to fall.
When it does,
find your way here. Kneel, dig, pray.
Plant it deep in the blood
soaked earth. Let your anguish be loud.
Even when the music of it cracks
every window for miles, stomp your feet bare

until exhaustion surrenders
to stillness. Roots will vine around your legs,
and then, you will begin
to grow firmer in the flourish. Your branches
will grow strong enough
to hold sparrows.

Lois Marie Harrod

THE CHILD WITH THE SMALL HEART

The child was born with a big chest and a small heart,
small and cold. The doctor said, there is not much
we can do. If she works hard, her heart may warm.

It happens to children and lambs: those given little,
accomplish, so the child was taught to believe.
Her little heart pumped double to provide for her

body while her parents worked triple to provide
for her siblings, there were three now,
all with normal-size hearts that didn't need

to work so hard. As she grew in wisdom and stature,
she met children like herself, the boy whose hands
were too small to pick up an acorn and the girl

who had pinpricks for eyes. They also worked hard
though she wasn't sure what they accomplished.
What would it be like, she wondered, to have

a large heart, to give off warmth and intimacy
instead of chill. Sometimes she contemplated
pictures of the Virgin, her enormous heart

pierced by seven swords. That must be difficult too,
she thought, forced to reveal so many wounds.
Better, perhaps, to have a small heart.

Matt W. Miller

TROUBLE

Just be a wandered off kid
at any airport and then shove

your arm into the hot black gap
of space where the conveyer belt

slips back under the edge
of the X-ray machine.

Make sure you're old enough
to know this is stupid,

young enough to have an arm
that can fit through but still get stuck

as the belt starts rubbing away
layers of skin. Now you're in it.

At first, do nothing. Your mom
is wiped out already travelling

with three sons all under the age
of five from Miami to Boston.

But then you will have to scream.
It will hurt. People's luggage

will shove and knock up against you.
That's when she'll freak, your mom,

hearing you cry, seeing you sucked
down by rubber, wheels, and metal.

Then the awful alarm. The lights.
The machine howling to a stop.

Somebody pulls your arm out.
There will be men in uniforms.

One will pour something stingy
onto the white pink brand you will

think looks like an eye right before
they bandage it up and help you all

to the gate before it's no longer
1978 and people start suing

over such things. To slip back out,
of trouble that is, wait a week or so.

Be a royal pain in the ass
big brother at a Burger King.

Steal your brother's toy or fries,
make him screech so mom

grabs you wild-eyed by the wrist
still wrapped in gauze and tape

and starting to yellow and stink.
Best to let her see the blood first,

after her squeeze rips the scab
and red streams through her fingers.

Then start wailing. It's still '78
so no one will call social services

but you'll get all the fries you can eat.
Plus, that look on her face.

Wesley Rothman

WHY MOTHER

Grandfather made certain to ingrain a bit of hate in my mother.
I've heard too often of the Black man who catcalled my mother.

A woozy tug captain hollers to his daughters before hitting
the hay; shouts and yells in his sleep until sighing *mother*.

She refuses to join our family photo, says lines have begun
to show, as if they were silent on her face before she lost Mother.

Don't drink the coffee, he'd startle his oldest, *you'll turn Black*.
She'd close her eyes, mutter *mother mother mother mother*.

Granddad passed a few months after I turned 12, died
many years earlier. At the funeral I stood near Mother.

These rebel roots wrap fingers round Daddy, snatch
at my heels heading west, for hope? Why mother?

Four years old, she's pulled to the lap of a man with no sons.
He slurs and she follows. Memories keep fighting mother.

In delivery, sweat beading her collarbone. *Wesley Paul*
to herself, *won't know my father, my sister, my mother*.

Müesser Yeniay

LAMENT

To be a woman
means being invaded, O mum!

they took of my everything

a woman took my childhood
a man, my womanhood...

God should not create woman
God does not know how to give birth

here, the ribs of all men
are broken

our neck is thinner than hair

men are carrying us
like a funeral on their shoulders

we have been under their feet

light like a feather
we flew from a world to an Adam

and my words are, oh mum!
their footprints....

Jennifer Martelli

NO FACE

When she has my father dial my number to say Liz is in the living room,
I don't say: *My sister is in Texas, you are in your home, by the ocean.*

She says she called to her, *Liz*, and when she looked up, my sister
had no face.   I say, *Like an egg?*

No, more like an oval hand mirror filled with smoke
she says, less frightened than by last

sundown's visitation: the seamstress in the cellar or the one before, the men
who call her thief or the one before, the girl with no legs who floats.

I picture my sister, her face covered all around
with gray scarves or with Saran wrap.

How, Ma? How no face? She starts to cry.
My father must have taken the phone from her, hangs it up nice and soft so

she won't get more scared and we wait
in our separate homes throughout sundown for full night.

Rage Hezekiah

HUNGER

I was waiting for a body unmine
to do the womanly work of swelling,
spilling open. I yearned to bleed
& burst, to render myself round,
curve into a circle. I feel the flesh

of my own form now, press
my palms against my breasts
as though I have earned them,
grown them from seed. My desire
will not shy, this source will nourish

another. But the mantra of your touch
reminds me: *Make love of yourself perfect*,
as though this is enough. If I was given
this gift, let me suckle somebody
who needs me, let me feed the living.

Colleen Michaels

THERAPEUTIC

I decide to tell my new nurse at the coumadin clinic
how she looks a bit like a poet whose lines stop traffic.
We google, and she agrees, something in the shoulders,
maybe around the eyes. She lets the guy with the walker
wait while we talk about poetry and heart failure.

Now when I go to give her my finger, let her test my blood,
be both kinds of patient, the room clots compassion, a poem.
I've learned what to do in a car accident, if things go bad.
She takes my hand, and tells me it might go bad,
but if it does, she says, we will know how to fix it.

Eve Packer

IF

i swim
far enuf,
long enuf,
do enuf
laps,
i'll shed
      my skin
maybe,
it will float
behind

      my kicking
         legs,
like used
      condom,
band-aid,
snake or
      sharkskin
fish-scales,
         i'll emerge,
after 2nd

         swim,
assets, capital,
cerebellum polished
intact
  bod &
    face
in
photoshop

Jennifer Jean

ANCHORING

For survivors of abuse and trafficking residing at The Anchor House for Boys.

With a fat eye roving,
this fat typhoon
swung every arm at this boat   called *The Big Buoy.*

And that wrecked kid took it
till he ducked
into a dip in the night like a mother   hug.

And before a swell rose under him,
he found a holding   ground.
Dropped his iron

like Saint Clement   dropped
into the Black Sea. He let go
a bulwagga, bower,

kedge, or kellick… Whichever
anchor—
its sharp dentes tucked

into the unknowable
sea floor, caught on that
"Presence

behind
the veil…"
so *The Big Buoy* could feel

the tug of
safety. Could bite at the harbored-life
like teeth bite   at a teat

to keep it.

January G. O'Neil

PRAYER

If at 4 a.m. you find yourself
awake and alone, curled up
in your half-empty bed under a flashlight's
small white light reading a poem,
little moon casting its aura across the page,

regret nothing:
not the clothes piled in the corner
not the drawers closed like caskets
the unpacked lunches, the pictures
quiet in their frames, the hats and gloves
by the door and the bodies they protect.
All that must be swept, bundled,
carried, and carted off to somewhere
else, only to return to the source of your
unmaking.

Regret nothing. Even as
a glimmer of yourself catches you
in the mirror, walk into the day
with your whole heart intact.
Walk into the center of everything.
Leave nothing in your wake.

Compassionate ACTION

Melissa Eleftherion

MAMA, TURN OUT THE LIGHT

The eggs are laid in the galleries
We wander, plucking faces from white walls
The yolk demands its attachment
The yolk broadcasts the feed

A nest of small beaks, a nest of plumes
In circles, circles
Wingless, a shiny cadence
Tufted f-stop heart
Lets light in, brave

The fight is feathery distance but we claw its shimmer of idea
A hologram that pops up strata with puffed chins and chest
The shooting gallery where we fire and fire
A high squealing wah wah wah

L.B. Williams

WHEN YOU WERE WILD
(after Louise Erdrich)

When you were far away
          snow fell green
Where trees were white hoary mountains
When three hundred year old men
          could sleep beneath eagles
          and become boys again
When I called to you
          my voice at first a whisper
When all the mandrake roots were
          taken from the earth
When a wind sighing chant
          brought you to me.

Holly Day

BUTTERFLY CAGE

when I was pregnant, all of my dreams
were about snakes. as much as I tried
to dream only about baby kittens, baby puppies
human babies, my nights would be filled
with twisting pythons gathered in knots
inside me, their slick skin undulating
in the dark, pushing and bumping as if
trying to find a way out.

friends without children would ask me
what it was like to be pregnant and I'd
have to lie. I was so worried that
imagining the baby inside me was a coiled serpent
in my stomach
meant that I was already a bad mother
meant something was wrong with my baby.

"It's like being a butterfly house," I'd say instead.
"I'm all full of fluttering butterflies." I'd put his or her hand
on my straining stomach as I spoke, whispering
"Can you feel them move? Can you feel it?

Isn't it wonderful?"

Wendy Taylor Carlisle

FOR AN OVERDUE BIRTH

He begins to swim as a shadow of himself, mostly tail, mooring to the imperative.
            When he is no longer one cell he is an always changing
spinal cord. Gills, rib, heart, lungs, the smallest feet emerge. He has his

instructions from both sides of the line to follow or ignore. The long hall of morning
                smells of old-fashioned cleaners: wax, Lysol, ammonia.
On the floor's shiny surface, one boot heel abrasion.

How heavy the everyday, with its hurtful light, how miraculous humans
            with their flimsy skin and breathing.

**

I bet I'm not the first woman to describe a man as a leopard in a neon suit
            not the first to conclude self-knowledge may come too late to do you any good.
On my Ozark hillside, houses have one leg shorter than the other.

Bobcat fever can carry off a tabby in 48 hours. I live
            with the false cough of I-have-no-answer.
His names slide against my knuckles and are gone.

Flaneur: an idle lounger, man about town.
            I would pray but the word beloved sticks in my teeth.

***

Begun as a trick of light and barbed wire, dust and pot,
            flash floods, surprising as an armadillo from under the porch, he comes.
I embrace all his parts.

Deborah Polikoff

LABOR

"…why is no woman's labor as famous as the death of Socrates?"
Louise Erdrich

No one told me that pain
is a thing, secretly ripening
in the womb like a strawberry
concealed in its bed of leaves.
No one told me that pain
is bountiful as the bunches
of grapes bowing down
the autumn arbor.
No one told me
that pain is a place
with boundaries clear
as the colors on a map, and no one
told me how many times
I could journey there and return
without moving.
No one told me that pain is a sound
I would become, cracking
like a sphere into
creation.

They said that the pain
would come in waves, but
no one told me that between
the waves is

silence, absolute
zero, a universe arrested
before its first
breath

Rosalie Calabrese

WHEN YOU WERE BORN

In the waiting room,
before I woke up,
the doctor told my mother,
"I had a boy" . . .
taking all the credit
while I, in a netherworld
induced by a shot of Sodium Pentothol
that made me tell the truth
of pain I wouldn't remember,
spewed out a stream of curses,
embarrassing even the nurses
who'd heard it all before.
That's what the doctor said,
but I'll never really know,
for I wasn't there
when you were born.

Elizabeth Deanna Morris Lakes

NEW MOTHER

I woke up to a doctor singing "Good morning!" He had on a head mirror and was rearranging his scalpels.

"Good morning," I told him.

"Congratulations!" he said. "You'll be a great mother."

"Mother!" I said, alarmed.

"Yes, mother," he told me. "You gave birth last night."

My hand shot to my vagina. Indeed, it was wider and looser. Stitches ran up one side, where I guessed the baby had torn me open.

"Stitches?" I asked. "Is the baby big?"

"Not really," said the doctor. "That was from the claws." A nurse bustled in with a bundle wrapped in a blue- and pink-striped blanket. She also sang good morning and handed me the bundle. I looked down and saw a lizard.

"How did I give birth to a lizard?" I asked her.

"That's a dragon," the nurse said. "Don't you even remember who you had sex with?"

"I didn't know I was even pregnant!" I let her know.

"Slut," she murmured and left. The dragon baby whined and nosed at my breast. I pulled down my gown and he latched on, teeth biting hard around the nipple.

"AGH!" I yelled.

"Suck it up!" said the doctor. "You can't let your baby starve. You've got to let it eat." The dragon baby suckled.

"Isn't there formula?" I asked. "A way to bottle feed?" The doctor sighed and left the room. The dragon baby finished eating and licked at the blood beading where his teeth had dug in. I tried to look at the bright side of things.

"What will I name you?" I mused out loud. The dragon baby offered up his paw. On it was a hospital bracelet. His name was Kenneth. I wouldn't even get to decide that.

Judith Skillman

CRADLE

Come now to the new place
where the large head waits,
bound and swaddled in flannel.
Come down as the birds plummet

from sky to nest. Circle back,
let the green rest, pace yourself
for the hundred years, the fluted edge,
the filigree tears falling

in a fountain from her breast
as she feels it empty.
Post partum, in the nursery,
a little muff of dust accumulates

against a headboard. See to the stain
of milk-spray, the tiny circles
she traces with her finger
as she nurses this new *Victor.*

Sara Emily Kuntz

BIRTH STORY
after Jean Painlevé's film L'Hippocampe

stomach tight and round
protruding proud
full of the fruits
of your devotion

and even convulsing
you look so graceful

tail curling and uncurling
head held high
like it is being pulled
on invisible reins

and out they come in spurts
little ghosts of yourself

Renee Beauregard Lute

BLUE PAPER, YELLOW MOONS IN PAINT

In the nighttime blue, we are an illustration
in my son's book.
Wrapped together in gray wool,
I nurse him until
he is milk-full and asleep.
I am already bruising
from the end of these blue paper nights.
From the end of the yellow moons
and the eventual last nursing.
Good endings untie me.
My eyes are already wet,
my chest is already a cave.

It is a moment of sadness,
it is a moment of joy.

Shanna Powlus Wheeler

MYSTIC AFFECTION

When the light shifted over my face, I woke to find you
wandering the hall and whispered, *It was the moon,*

because you were confused by dreams. *Come back to bed,*
where we drifted to our separate darknesses, while our child,

who has begun to acquaint the painted orbs and crescents
in her thick-paged books with their bright referent,

slept in her crib across the hall. *Moon, moon!* she cries
when she spots it through a window. Searching the sky

in daylight, she sees against the blue its slight print.
When it hides behind clouds, she opens books, finds it

gracing brush-stroked skies or masquerading
as the gray underside of a mallard duck's wing.

She points to the roused bird, *O moon,* then kisses the page.

Virginia Petrucci

BREAKFAST

You
Tucked under my arm
The water is still
Too hot, so
We wait

You
Wrapped ape and airy
Around my waist
Impatient fists
I mix the oatmeal

Sit you
Prop you
Kiss you

Small spoon strikes
Quick opening
Your little gape

Cooing back at me
Baby bird tongue tastes
The bowl goes flying
A revolt

Sandra Kohler

KATIE SAYS YES

At not quite two, Katie has begun to say
yes. To say yes as solemnly as if her yes
were the confirmation of the state of things,
the affirmation of her assent to the universe.
She says yes to questions, to statements, to
observations about weather, about whether,
what and how, when and if. About why.

She says no like a two-year old, but she
says yes like a sage, an elder, a philosopher,
a mystic. Yes, she says. Yes, I agree. It is so.
I understand it is so. I consent, I allow, I
profess, I know. I know: not no, yes. Is there
anything in my life to which I can say yes
the way she does? Perhaps Katie herself.

Lisa Wiley

TAKING MY 8-YEAR-OLD DAUGHTER TO HEAR SEAMUS HEANEY

She thinks he's like Papa —

snow white mop, ruddy cheeks.
He gives away secrets, shares sparks

from his life that inspire the work.
She sits straighter.

His granddaughter Avie flies a kite;
she wants to fly one too,

up to the roof beams of this lofty ceiling.
She peels potatoes

at the kitchen basin with Seamus
and his mother Sunday mornings

while all his siblings have gone to Mass.
Tomorrow maybe she'll find poetry

at our farmer's sink —
her hands and mine peeling potatoes.

Ana C.H. Silva

AT THE NATIONAL MUSEUM OF THE AMERICAN INDIAN, COLUMBUS DAY

Mia enters.
Are kids allowed?
I follow her. The fluorescent
lights are a diffuse glow through canvas.
Hand painted riders on burnt red and blue mosaic horses
black ponytails wrapped tight in grey cloth line the round. Is this a real tipi?
With small fingertips Mia touches each rider's face   each horse's face. Do I stop her?

Mia sees
through the open
circle at the top   where air
sun and wind would come in. She is quiet.
Museum ceiling hovers over the top   painted an
awful taupe   but she sees the whole sky   watches a cloud pass
before she speaks her story like a dozen people sit at her feet. To keep us close
she whispers. Ssss sounds and chchchch sounds flit through her story butterflies circling dust

in sunlight.
Each scrape of her throat
is a scold of jays. Mia moves her small
hands in the air. They make a triangle above her
head   break apart   her fingers a firm flutter. Each wave of her finger
a host of raindrops   her soft footfalls a herd of antelope a rider who lost his horse.
Or maybe I'm guessing   a single large animal on its own   moving roughly across the land.

Kristin Agudelo

THE WORLD OF FORMS

Plato would say the tire swing on my oak
is but a shadow of some Great Black Circle

Its summery rubber smell, a half-remembered resin
squeezed from the Celestial Tree

Smooth treads reflecting mellow May
the palest glaze of Light unquenched.

My boy simply grasps the twisted Cord of Life
kicks his grubby feet up, and pushes

Off, cackling, his shadow dashing
over the newly-turned Spring earth.

Susie Berg

BEACH STREET BRIDGE, OGUNQUIT, MAINE

One by one we grow as old as our brothers,
earn your gentle push from the bridge.
We dance like bait on fishing lines,
holler glee under a halo of Maine sun
into tidewater
depth-tested with rocks and sticks.

From birth we know
this is not risk, but considered leap;
how the shallows on the river side of the beach
are footsteps from the bottomless Atlantic.

No barrier warms this surf:
these are our waters to brave.
I taste salt the day my own boys
breach the edge.
You take photos from the dune.

Patrice Boyer Claeys

OUR TWELFTH YEAR AT THE POOL

In the cupped bowl of the pool's belly
with walls speckled and textured,
their color softening the deeper we dove,
we looked up at the wavering striations, feeling
the silence that sharpened our otherworldly
sense of where we were, suspended.
Through the comedy of goggles we sought
each other in buoyant mime, flat hand
finding flat hand, palm to palm
in the water's calm, then pushed away,
my mass raised aloft while your
tapering body kicked down deeper,
a young frog's with legs extended,
bobbed hair an areola flared
around a face wreathed with bubbles.
On the edge of womanhood you swam
with slow flashes of trapped light,
bright spheres flattening to capsules
of rising air. The purple sash
around your slender hips rippled
with each kick, a waving reed.
Breaking the surface, we gulped air,
then down again, resisting the water's
lift. Over and over we mirrored
each other, fitting our hands
together, yours almost my size,
fingers splayed as you pushed away,
your form uncoiling, streaming out,
receding as your supple limbs unfurled,
a trail of molten silver in your wake.

Andrea Potos

ALMOST EIGHTEEN

I am loitering in memory:
lasertag parties and storybook ballet,
her math facts and chapter books, the first
Magic Treehouse she devoured on her own.
Impatience and relish
when I had to lay beside her
until she fell asleep each night.

I am standing at the dock:
silver water swirling
between us, my girl
aiming toward the widening spaces.
Already, I can barely see
the wave of her handkerchief.

Vickie Iorio

WORDS OF COMPASSION

On this first day of spring
the late afternoon sun is a warm moon
on my back soothing the panic of old bones

The Ruth Stone poem I am reading
starts *On this first day of spring*
she is looking for a compass
to direct her widowhood   I can relate to a woman left alone
with children to raise

My daughter has gone to Italy
Ciao, Bella   raise them right   watch their flight
she will run the maratona di roma   feel the pull of
dead relatives at her feet

She emailed me about the beauty
called me mommy   usually I'm just ma or nothing at all
called me mommy   pins my heart   mosaics my soul

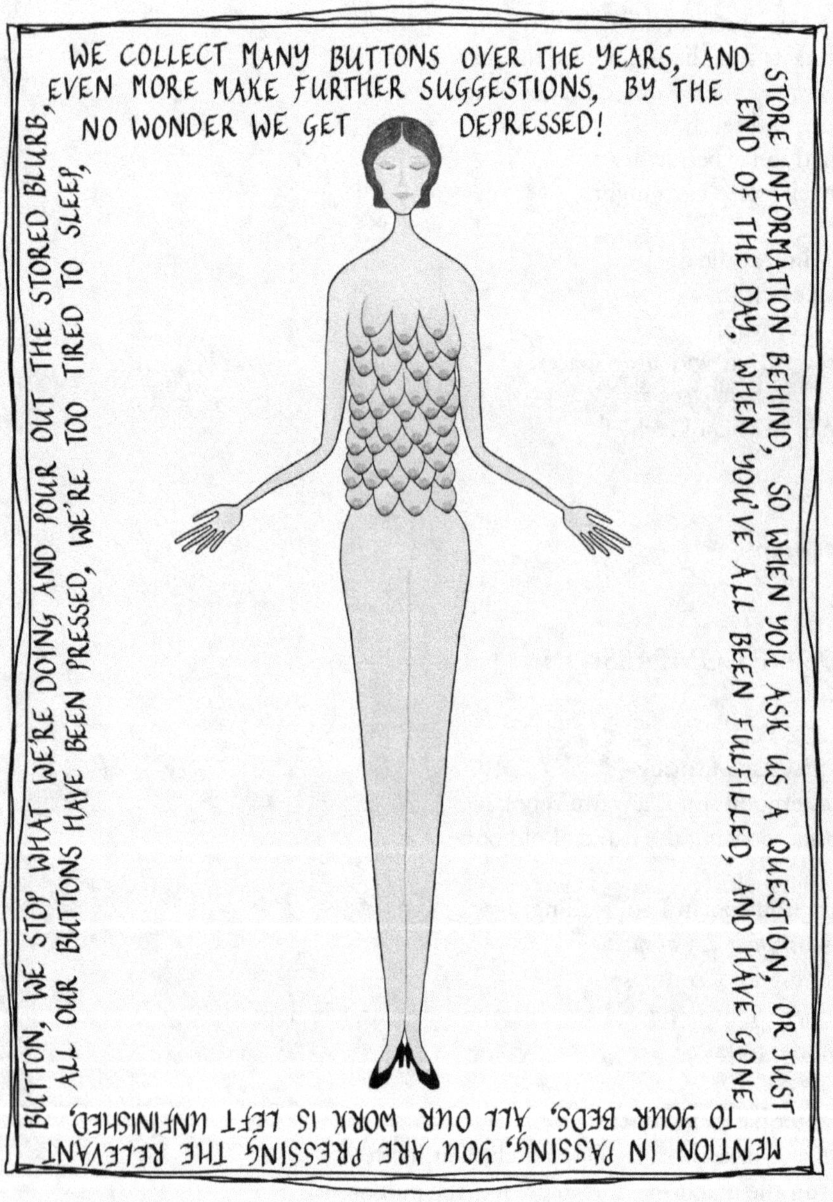
WE COLLECT MANY BUTTONS OVER THE YEARS, AND
STORE INFORMATION BEHIND, SO WHEN YOU ASK US A QUESTION, OR JUST
MENTION IN PASSING, YOU ARE PRESSING THE RELEVANT
BUTTON, WE STOP WHAT WE'RE DOING AND POUR OUT THE STORED BLURB,
EVEN MORE MAKE FURTHER SUGGESTIONS, BY THE
END OF THE DAY, WHEN YOU'VE ALL BEEN FULFILLED, AND HAVE GONE
TO YOUR BEDS, ALL OUR WORK IS LEFT UNFINISHED,
ALL OUR BUTTONS HAVE BEEN PRESSED, WE'RE TOO TIRED TO SLEEP,
NO WONDER WE GET DEPRESSED!

Anna Lawson, "Artemis Ephesos"

Anna Lawson, "Kali"

Hilary King

TO THE PUPS WHO RAISED US

We learn to change the wet, reeking paper,
to give eye drops or ear drops,
to get up in the middle of the night for someone else.
The first family we make on our own
rises out of impulse or accident,
responsibility not yet a color
we know how to wear.
The dog found at the gas station,
the cat left behind by a roommate.

We learn love over the years, saying
Can I bring my dog?
You're not allergic to cats, are you?
Oh, the dog's great with the baby.

Then, in the middle of what we thought
was a long walk, they suddenly lie down.
We learn then how to end a life,
the medicine, the mess,
the long wait in hard chairs.
We won't grow old together,
another idea they tame for us,
the pups who raised us.

Molly Howes

GIVING BIRTH TO STEP-CHILDREN

My bones remember the babies I bore. My misshapen skin held their folded forms. Afterwards, I listened to snuffly, uneven breathing and thin wailing in the dark hours, to learn my baby son's ways. I held my breath, to discover what delighted my toddler daughter. They left my body's cave long ago, but when my big children reach to me now, my hands and my voice know what comforted them when they were small.

With my stepchildren, I didn't get to have the intimate experience of pregnancy or the celebration of adoption day. I, like most, became a stepparent at my wedding. The four of them, my children and his children, held the vine-covered supports of the hoopah, all of us dressed up and anxious.

I never knew the babies his children had been. Instead of snuggling in the midnight rocking chair, we had uprooted households. Instead of private knowing, we had unhappy grandparents. Instead of my familiar hand, they longed for the other mother. The real one. The one who had learned their baby needs.

In our case, the real mother had died.

That word, "step," signals the extra distance that will always be between us – at least one step. Often it has felt more like a chasm. A stepmother is a threadbare rag in the winter: I have so little of what they want most. In addition to the mistakes I've authored myself, I have been an unrelenting, flashing sign of their loss: I'm *here here here*. She's *gone gone gone*. Eyes squeezed tight, they hold onto the one who's gone and erase me for a minute. They have wanted so badly not to see me.

They have also wanted not to love me; loving me could mean they were moving on in a terrible, profoundly sad way. I know now that their distance and distaste, highlighting my faults with neon markers, never had much to do with me. But their cold resistance sometimes felt like it would chill me forever.

Regardless of how they feel about me, though, what I feel for them turns out to be mother love. Furthermore, I know exactly when I became the parent of my stepdaughter, when I "gave birth" to our relationship. She was thirteen. We sat in the front row and listened to her pray the Blessings, sing her Torah portion like an angel, and deliver the insightful talk she'd prepared. Her voice clear, she shone with intelligence and strength. Suddenly, I realized I could no longer tell if her beauty and grace were objectively true. Suddenly, I only viewed her through the fierce, shaded lens of a parent. From then on, I knew I belonged to her, even if she didn't belong to me.

With my stepson, the labor was longer and harder. When his blame blazed unbearably and my pain spasmed into misery, I'd wanted only to push him out. I'd hide in the big flowered chair next to the attic, hurt by his displaced unkindness more than I could take. At those moments, I admitted defeat. I thought, *his going to college can't come soon enough*. Then, one winter, when a blizzard buffeted our house and the fireplace became our only heat source, we pulled the couch close to it. He sat next to me. On that day of loud wind and warm fire, we reached the end of a painful conversation with more mutual understanding than we had started it with. His flushed fury settled and I knew I would always try again with him. I can not be his mother, but I will always be his parent.

Now, they both have stretches of trust and connection with me, although those times can feel fragile, like a young child on unsteady legs. Learning our way with each other takes so much time. I hope they will continue the path we've started. I hope they will let others love them well and long. I hope they will have the chance to embrace children, regardless of how the children arrive in their lives.

Deborah L. Blicher

LEAP OF FAITH

The little boy I hope will become my son lines up his scuffed shoes on the edge of the sandbox, gauging the distance to the ground. It's sixty degrees out, but like all the children I have seen in this Russian city, he's overdressed to my American eye. Between his striped, knitted cap and puffy blue coat, I can hardly see his face. We speak different languages, but as far as I can tell, he hates me.

The boy, whose name in Misha, is two and a half, with feathery blond eyebrows and merry eyes. Four days ago, my husband Peter and I met him and his sister at their orphanage. The children smiled up at us in the entryway decorated with finger paintings. When their caregiver Anna introduced us--as friends, not yet as parents--they giggled and scrambled down the hall. Smitten, we followed. They rolled trucks at us across the living room carpet. We had a pretend tea-party on the floor and a real one at the table. When Misha vaulted onto the couch and unfurled his body into a magnificent headstand, Anna instructed him to come down. Like every two year old in the world, he refused, so she carried him to the time-out chair.

Over the last three days, the children have sought increasing intimacy with us: holding our hands, daring us to chase them, imitating our English. Yesterday, they ran down the hall in their socks to greet us with outstretched arms. This morning, however, our final visit, they seem subdued. Misha's sister Katja gravely takes Peter's hand and leads him to the playground sandbox. Misha doesn't follow. I walk him to the jungle-gym, which he climbed yesterday with joyful grace. Today he climbs grudgingly. He lets his fingers slip and watches me catch him, and he squawks if I stand too close. I feel he's wondering both, "Will you keep me safe?" and "Will you give me freedom?"

I decide to try the swing, which he loved yesterday. He faces away from me as I carry him and slumps with apathy when I push him. From behind the swing, I ask whether he's all right: "*Te harasho?*" He turns one round ear towards me but won't reply. When I walk around to the front of the swing, he searches my face a long time.

Back at the sandbox, Peter and Katja have built a row of sandcastles. Peter is earnestly and slowly counting them for her in English. The expression on Katja's sharp-chinned face suggests she'd like to have him committed. When I set Misha beside her, he turns his back on me and starts singing with a songbird's loveliness. Then he extends a flattened palm and wipes out the sand-castle I'm building.

Finally I understand. Someone's explained to the children that Peter and I want to adopt them, taking them away from the life they know. Misha is not angry with Peter because Peter won't replace a father figure, but he's angry with me because I'll replace Anna, the only mother he knows.

His loss staggers me.

My instinct is to offer love and wait. I begin by heaping up sand-castles for him to smash.

He does.

Soon, it will be time for us to go inside. Peter and I will remove the children's coats in the entryway and line up their shoes next to ours. We'll share cake and tea. Katja will pour out pretend tea. Then Peter and I will sign documents stating our intention to adopt.

I stand up, brushing off sand. Peter scoops up Katja. Misha climbs onto the edge of the sandbox and gauges the distance to the ground. I don't reach out to help him. I know he doesn't trust me, the usurper.

He slides his eyes to me for a moment. I resist every urge. Then he puts his hand into mine, grips hard, and jumps.

Wendy Jones Nakanishi

LOVING

"You must not use paper diapers. It is a nuisance to wash cloth ones, but they bond you to the baby. If you use disposable ones he can sense, even in his first months, your indifference, your unwillingness to make an effort for him."

"You need to begin wearing a maternity *obi* as soon as possible."

Emmie's sister-in-law, Kuniko, held out an example. It was more like a long white sash than the tight buttoned garment she had been expecting.

Kuniko stroked the cloth softly: "The baby will feel comforted, and your lower abdomen needs the support as your belly gets heavier."

"Please talk gently to your baby throughout the day as you go about your work."

"You should try to avoid any sort of stress."

"I beg you not to ride a bicycle after your fifth month."

Emmie sat, a tiny blonde figure shielding a slightly rounded tummy with her hands, on a sofa as her Japanese husband's mother and sister bombarded her with advice and admonitions.

They're already assuming I'll have a boy, she thought. *I wonder if I'll disappoint them.* She sighed heavily.

"You need calcium," her mother-in-law observed, holding out a small blue dish. Emmie swallowed hard. Even the smell made her feel sick. The dish was full of tiny grey fish. They were whole, with eyes as small as pinpricks. The fish had been mixed with mayonnaise and a hint of soy sauce to make them palatable.

The old woman smiled as she offered Emmie a pair of wooden chopsticks and said in a cajoling voice: "Please eat it all. It will make your son's bones hard and strong."

After the first tentative bite, Emmie was relieved to find that, apart from the texture -- that feeling of crunching bones with every mouthful -- the fish, with their dressing of creamy saltiness, were palatable.

But Emmie had to struggle to repress an impulse to jump up and run away. All her pride in being a university lecture, her enjoyment of the status it afforded her in Japan, now seemed irrelevant. She felt like an animal kept for breeding purposes. The joyousness that had overwhelmed her when the doctor had announced she was expecting seemed to be dissipating with every word her in-laws said to her. Kenji's family knew nothing of her real thoughts and feelings. For all their obviously genuine concern, she felt used. Was she sublimated to a flesh-and-blood factory that would deliver an heir for them?

Emmie was perfectly aware they were desperate for a male to carry on the line. Kenji's elder sister Kuniko had only produced two daughters. Kenji was the last of the main line of the Ogawa family. If he had no son, who would inherit the family farm?

Kenji sat by Emmie's side. She let one hand stray to her side, and he surreptitiously squeezed it.

He had asked if they could visit his parents' house, only five minutes' walk from their own, on their return from the hospital. He posed it in the nature of a favor. He said he was fully aware Emmie would find it an ordeal. She was such a private person. He knew she wanted to keep her secret to herself, hugging it as she wanted to hug her future child.

"But we live in Japan," Kenji had said gently. "Maybe it's different in America, but here, family is all important. We can't *not* tell my parents you're expecting a child."

Emmie had nodded. Miserable.

"And you'll probably have to go back to work months after the birth. Who will look after it, until it's one or two and can enter nursery school? My mother, I imagine."

Emmie bit back angry words. *What if I don't want to go back to work? Maybe I can be a full-time mother.*

But she knew this wasn't an option. She worked at a small private Japanese university and was the main breadwinner. Her husband was a farmer who worked hard, all day, every day, but whose income was tiny in comparison to hers.

After ten years' residence in Japan, Emmie had become fluent in the language. At this point, she regarded it more as a curse than a blessing. Naturally, she would understand everything his family said to her, and she knew she was expected to muster up at least a semblance of acquiescence to all their suggestions about managing her pregnancy.

Suddenly Emmie's mother-in-law knelt before her and held out her hands.

"My dear daughter-in-law," she said, her eyes filling with tears. "We are so grateful you have joined our family."

Emmie was abashed to see that Kuniko had also knelt down, her head bowed in agreement.

Emmie suddenly had to blink back tears. Her own mother was dead. It was unbearably touching that this diminutive woman with her formal manners who had always seemed to treat her as an exotic stranger was humbling herself before her and inviting her affection.

Loving, Emmie thought. It's nothing you can plan for. She suddenly felt a great surge of it for her husband and his family and for the new life that soon would be joining them.

PEOPLE WHO JUST LOVE KIDS

Elle and I are sitting in the deli downstairs waiting for our breakfast specials. Jeff and Arin are upstairs packing a few books; we've ordered breakfast specials for them, too.

"Hiya, Buddy," calls Elle, to yet another person in the building whom she knows and I don't. Elle and Arin have mentioned Buddy a few times. I think he works at the bar; sometimes he gives the kids quarters.

I look up and there's Buddy, about six feet of him, maybe 55 years, maybe 225 pounds. And I just have a feeling he's one of those people who just-loves-kids and who, in his youth, said I just-love-kids-but-not-my-own. "Hey!" he goes. "How's my girlfriend"

"Foine," Elle grins.

"Can I have some of those curls?" he teases.

"Uh-UH." Elle is still grinning.

"Hey, where's your brother?"

"He's upstairs – oh, here he is." For Jeff and Arin are sliding into the opposite side of the booth.

"Hi, Arin" says Buddy.

"Hi," answers Arin.

Then Buddy turns to me. "Hello, Mother," he says.

"Hi," I answer. "The name is Marion." I kind of feel like adding "or Dr. Cohen, whichever you prefer." I don't like to resort to titles but I also don't like being called Mrs. Cohen, or even Mother, not in that way. And there are certain leering types to whom I don't like to say "call me Marion". So sometimes it's hard, or impossible, to know what to do.

At this point Arin crawls under the table to visit with Elle and me. "That's right," says Buddy, "give Mother a hug. Give Mother a biiig hug."

Now, why do I just hate this? What does it make me feel degraded? It's the tone of his voice, for one thing. I'm pretty sure I'm not imagining it. It's as though he's making fun of the whole idea of motherhood. As though he's satirizing it, as though he thinks he's above it. Almost as though he's *monitoring* it.

"Ja go swimming today?" Buddy nudges Elle.

"Uh-uh," answers Elle.

"Hey" – turning to me (and not Jeff, the father) – "why don'tcha join a pool for her?"

Now I *know* I'm not imagining it. He *is* criticizing me, for not "joining a pool for her". I know that look and it is very definitely not just-kidding.

"I'd be happy to join a pool," I answer, "if they were free. But they cost too much."

Now, the following *you know* I'm not imagining. "Maybe," says Buddy, "maybe if ya cooked 'em breakfast upstairs instead of eating downstairs all the time, you could afford to join a pool."

Now, there might be a twinkle in his eye, but I can't see it. And, smiling wisely but sadly, I reflect: It is very definitely an axiom of life – an axiom both in the sense that it's a basic principle and in the sense that I can't prove it – that people who just-love-kids are very often people who just-hate-mothers. To put it more accurately, albeit with less impact, there is a certain *class* of people who just-love-kids and who also just-hate-mothers. These people are probably usually people who don't have kids themselves, but who knows? Strange things happen.

For this class of people there's some kind of twisted logic to just-hating mothers. If you love children, you want to protect them from their enemies, people who spoil their fun, and who might cause them to be occasionally "bad". After all, if a child is bad there must be a Reason. And what better Reason to pick on than the mother?

Also, people who just-love-kids are people who want kids to just-love-*them* so they probably feel in competition with the mothers. Or downright jealous. They know darm well that the kids whom they so adore usually love their mothers more than them, and they know that no kid will ever love them in that way. "Go to mother, now," they say, or "here's some delicious candy – if your mother says it's okay" and "*I'm* not going to scold her; that's her mother's job" (and not the father's).

So I'm smiling wisely but sadly, and this is one of those times when I'm not gonna fight it. I'm not in the mood this time. So I simply say "We're moving and our kitchen is all packed up." But a minute later I'm no longer smiling wisely but sadly; I'm frowning wisely but sadly.

Kimberly Dark

Mother is a way to turn the light on
when you walk into the room
mother is a way to call the dogs
only be careful - because too many dogs
may come and run you over,
eat your meat and chew your bones
mother is a way to look in the mirror
a way to remember what the sunrise looks like
even when you're indoors
even when it's night time
even if you're down deep in a hole
mother is 10 AM and 2 PM like clockwork
mother is chaos
all things in their opposites
all things trapped in their opposites
mother is the white curtains lightly fluttering
around the bedroom window in a breeze
mother is a moment when the moon rises
you look up and simultaneously feel a hand
around your shoulder squeezing a little bit too hard
mother is gentle with others and cannot find
the way the forgive herself with you
mother craves you
wants nothing more than you
wants you to forgive her
and can't believe you already did
years ago, so long ago
mother's body stiffens up like a fork
if you try to hug her
there's nothing you can do to please her
there's nothing nothing ever again
mother is like the sunset
full of colors, like someone
painted an ocean of all the colors
all around you, everywhere you look
soon it will go black
and you'll be alone, blinking
wondering how it all happened
so fast.

Emily R. Blumenfeld

MATERNAL PRACTICE

Every day I practice
leaning into sounds resting on
your eyes, kissing your wings
while holding you close.

Some moments my kiss
spins too tight. My fingertips
try to knit lace without holes,
touch a butterfly with a whole hand.

Over and over I practice
keeping my worries out of
your sight, capturing my fears
wandering into your dreams.

Anna Lowe Weber

MY DAUGHTER'S MOUTH

Which I have chosen to kiss,
again and again, because my
own mother never did. No
lack of love in our family,
but no kisses either, and so
I bring my lips to hers day
after day, morning and night.
I love you—smack. Good
morning—smack. It always
surprises me, how wet they are.
I should see it coming by now—
slippery as pond rock, glassy-thick
with an overcoat of toddler saliva.
But I am not repulsed. I tell
myself this as I lean in for
another big one, plant my mouth
right against hers. Her mouth
so eager it shames me when
I pull away first.

Atoosa Grey

DAUGHTER

Sometimes I wrap my arms
around you tight, and know
there will come a day
when you no longer
sneak into my bed at night
and curl your sleepy bones
against my sorrow
and make it small again.

Jamie Lynn Heller

I DENIED HER

I denied her
ice cream cones for many years.
Memories of anticipated sweetness
landing on hot, ant sprinkled sidewalks
kept me insisting hers
would be served in a bowl.

I denied her
the lesson of licking softly, consciously
planning how to tackle a bump and balance
the whole on its precarious perch,
how to anticipate melting, the satisfaction

of licking the back of a hand
to get a runaway drop,
earning the crunch of the cone,
using her tongue
to get the last drops buried deep.

Maria Mazziotti Gillan

HOW MANY HOURS

"The world is too much with us; late and soon,
Getting and spending we lay waste our powers;" William Wordsworth

How many hours have I spent pushing a shopping cart
through Pathmark or Bradlees or Target? How many days
when the children were small did I place Jennifer in the baby seat
and John in the shopping cart and walk through the aisles
of Bradlees because the walls of that tiny apartment in married
student housing were closing in on me, because Dennis was
in grad school and busy and I had the children and I was so lonely
that I walked those aisles to use up the time in the day
that seemed endless.

There was nothing I wanted in all those stacks
of objects—toasters and towels and blenders and sheets,
but I had to keep walking, counting off the minutes
and even in the grocery store where I had to go
because I needed to buy food for my family, even there
I felt the minutes of my life draining away
while I waited in line and tried to keep
the children entertained. Oh, all those endless hours,
the grumpy looks on the faces of the people in those aisles,
those people waiting as though
they were trying to fill the Grand Canyon inside them.
In these tacky aisles there is nothing I want or need
except this daily excursion that I use to prove
to myself that I can survive these mundane days,
time like a dark tunnel I must travel through
to get to the other side.

Today, so many years later I can feel Jennifer as a baby
in my arms, John with his hand on my chest while I read
a book to him. Yes, I loved them and love them still,
and I remember my mother telling me that I would come to long
for the time when my children were hanging on my skirt, and she
was right. How quickly our children grow and disappear
into their new lives. How much we long to have them back

smelling of baby powder and shampoo, but time refuses
to move backwards. Now, I try
to avoid shopping in big box stores, where the past slaps me
in the face, the memory of those forlorn moments so long ago,
when I walked the aisles with my children in the cart
and wished for something or someone to save me.

Artress Bethany White

MUMMIES LIKE THIS (IN MOMENTS LIKE THESE)

So much of mothering
is truth
you cannot divulge
over glasses of wine
with the girls,
unspeakable
weariness
that makes you
put dirty dishes
atop clean
in the dishwasher drawer
no energy left to separate
new from old
wheat from chaff,
that same day
going pantyless,
a wisp of silken decency
forgotten
on the bathroom counter
forsaking
your own butt
yet again
in your haste
to spit-shine
the children
get them out the door
in some semblance of order
to preserve your good name.

Judy Kronenfeld

BABYSITTING INSTRUCTIONS FOR THE OLDER GRANDPARENT

Swiftly retie your grandson's sneakers
while he insists *I do it
myself!* Snuggle him into
the car seat, and buckle it
(don't awkward-angle
that doddery knee!),
give him plush pup
and his sippy cup
and whisk him from day-care
lickety-split singing *wheels
of the bus wheels of the bus,*
saying *yes!* to every gleeful *TRUCK!*
while the leaves blaze gold
and crisp and drop
without a sound, without
a sound, and a muster of crows
flaps over the trees.

Praise the tiny tupperware cups
you must fill with raisins or
teddy grahams, and praise the lunch-box
you have to find,
and the bedtime story you have to
read, and the desperate cries
for a third from the crib, *Snowy Day!
Snowy Day!,* before the child plummets
to sleep.

Praise falling into the guest bed, exhausted,
with granddad, exhausted, who ran
repeatedly to the slide in the playground
to grab the flame-cheeked, careening boy,
and cleaned and diapered
the fusser's bottom and hustled him
into nighttime footies, and hunted down
that rascal blue cow.

Praise sleepy caressing
and sleepy forgetting warm flesh
will be ash, and gravity rules,

and granddad's beating heart's
precarious,
when nothing's
the matter
In the Night Kitchen,
or anywhere.

Lori Levy

IN THE GARDEN OF GRANDMA

Something tempts him in the garden. Armor-plated, black,
so small he almost misses it, crawling in the soil
where he's digging. He scoops with his shovel,
plucks it from the dirt: a roly poly in his palm.
His sister inches closer, peering at his hand.
She is one, he is four. We stare,
the three of us intrigued—though I, their grandma,
focus more on *them* than *it*.
What is it that makes him poke and prod
while she blows kisses at the bug?
The roly poly curls into a ball.
They watch, seduced, waiting for another trick.
It's knowledge that they crave: what is this armadillo bug?
What can it do? He flicks it to the ground,
where, upside down, it wriggles all its legs.
She smiles, *wows.* He presses with his finger,
pushing it deeper into the earth.

Pill bug, potato bug, roly poly—buried, but not dead.
The children play, I do what grandmas do.
Maybe the tiny thing is hungry, I suggest.
Or needs a home.
The boy stops squashing to consider this,
then helps me make a bed of leaves.
What is it now that softens his hand
to set the creature *gently* down
and offer it a blade of grass?
His sister—charmed to see it straighten and stir—
blows another kiss.

Beth Bosworth

THE STORY OF THE FOOD

The one-year-old girl is telling the story of her meal.

The grandmother is listening.

The girl is strapped into her red high chair, a geometric, wooden chair whose straps fit over the girl's shoulders and clasp at her waist.

The grandmother leans over to slice a lengthy strand of spinach.

The girl puts one strand into her mouth and scrunches her nose.

It seems to the grandmother that the girl has just discovered her own nose. She makes this scrunched face, like a fake smile, and she has more than once rubbed at her nose and once picked it with a delicate forefinger.

The girl is telling the story of her meal. How to tell this story in words? Perhaps a morsel of chicken has wandered off. Perhaps the potato salad (the girl doesn't seem to care for it) is standing guard or counting its blessings. Then again, the form of this meal might take musical shape. It might have stanzas and a different refrain for each listener. To the grandmother, the refrain has to do with another baby a long time ago, and how privileged the grandmother had felt, in that younger time, to feed and wash and clothe that other baby. This sense of privilege had to do with her own childhood and certain feelings of taint, of being tainted. To the one-year-old girl, whose song it is, the refrain has an entirely different meaning.

But perhaps the story of the meal has more to do with appearances, with the size and shape and number of chicken morsels, the seasoning on potatoes, the halving of grapes—green grape halves that the girl pops into her mouth one after another.

The next morning, the grandmother has planned to leave without waking anyone. It is very early—hardly breakfast time. From the other side of their bedroom door, however, she hears the little family, mother, father, girl, the father's voice rising and falling and the girl letting out an occasional, exuberant cry. The grandmother knocks. When a sleepy voice says, "Okay," she takes the word for permission to enter. The baby crouches near the bed and the father is only now sliding into his pants and buckling them.

"Excuse me," the grandmother says, kneeling to greet the girl, who eyes her solemnly.

Driving home, the grandmother hears her cellphone ringing. She glances at the number and drives on through the rain. She thinks about a beloved dog who has recently died, leaving her with this new life on her hands. Always, as she turned into the driveway, the dog would have leaped up, would have reached his paw onto her shoulder.

The grandmother calls her daughter right back. "Did you call me?" she asks.

"I called you by accident," the daughter says in a high-spirited tone.

The rain is still falling as the grandmother hurries toward the house. Among other resolutions, she has decided to insert this term, "butt-dialing," into future conversations.

Once inside, she tries to explain to her husband about the story of the food, but the girl seems to have told it in a language that doesn't bear repeating.

Gail Ghai

THE ORANGE BOX OF BIRD THINGS

When Barbara and I found the baby bird,
dead as yesterday, we wept to our mother
working in her flower garden,

working as the hot August sun started its cider
climb She stroked the soft brown crest.
All life dies, she said gently.

And we howled for the bird,
for ourselves, for the earth,
the way you do at four and five

when your heart believes,
your heart loves
even the air.

You need to bury it, she urged as she
dug her trowel under a red gladiola.
A funeral! Barbara and I dueted

scrambling to the backdoor.
The bustle in a house
The morning after death

We fought over the paper coffin.
Salada tea carton or *Graham* wafer package.
We filled the orange box with bird things:

scarlet strings, feathers, our budgie's seeds.
We buried it next to the garden fence
where sunflowers towered

in their yellow happiness.
Will it go to heaven, I asked my mother.
Does it have wings? She replied.

Angels! We chorused in our small Catholic voices.
Angels, with light luminous bodies,
divine messengers,

harbingers of devotion,
change,
resurrection.

Chelsea Dingman

DOG DAYS

I can't stop the dawn
to catch my breath. You expand
while my eyes rest, as if you're taking

on water. I'm unsure of your best
interests, so vast, your childhood
is a foreign country, this language

I struggle to master. An accident
is in the road up ahead
unless each mile is driven

with careful attention
to the signs, an eye
on the miles behind. I drive

to follow you, it seems, rather
than little steps I remember
at my heels. My burden

is a landmark, a turn.
Your life becomes the road
away, quiet sores I carry.

E.J. Antonio

THIS IS HOW WE GROW INTO WOMEN

> *Billie Holiday's burned voice*
> *had as many shadows as lights… Rita Dove*

Dear Wanda:

I didn't know you, but I hugged you that evening at the Black Renaissance reading. Hugged you long and hard, almost dancing in the memory of the lyric of your voice. Your voice, a lilt of southerly cadence, snapped me back to my grandmother's pulpit, back to when we were trained to listen and be still. Just be still and absorb the legacy. Yes I hugged you, Wanda Coleman. Hugged you hard, the way my 12-year old mind hugged Billie Holiday. I inhaled the embers of you as easily as…

the frigid smoke of her voice swept me into ache
my eyes closed / absorbed her burnt orange moans
seedin' my skin / fenced in and overgrown

this is how we grow into women

holdin' the mournful splinters of a woman's life
in our make-believe roses / her voice a bush beaten
down in winter's snow / pierced / my eyes have learned

this how we grow into gut-bucket women / take no shit women
                    do you see any chocolate diamonds on these hands, Wanda?

learnin' the nuances of crushed songs / my ears
recognize on every twist of barb an experience carried in each
creakin' note / the unpaid day tumbling into other unpaid days

this how we grow into blues women carryin' traditions
                    learnin' to step over sidewalk cracks - full rivers of dog piss
                        carryin' on under our breath holdin' talismans

switchblade and razor in brassiere cups
lye, sugar and bleach stitched in seams
pistol and cast-iron skillets tucked firm in garters

This is how we grow, Wanda; how we learn to wear our faces inside out
while our lips smile, our voices cajole, our eyes burn, and we learn to run our blades along the
spine of anything that will break us. Mad hatter women lookin' for chauffer-men… handy-

men…Cheshire cat piano playin' men… jumpin' out every woman's window on Monday mornin'.
This is the back beat she left us, and I wish I really could've hugged Billie the way I hugged you
that day, Wanda.

this is how we grow into women…

I still hear the southerly lilt of your voice
  your "ain't no salt water pearls hangin' round this neck, honey" voice

and my intuition swells up from the bone
tells me my own stingin' nettles will sprout in spring
wrackin' my skin a ruined field

forever irrigated by Billie's frigid smoky voice
I'm always waitin' / waitin' for her
to christen me woman

Puma Perl

ALL THAT AUTHENTICITY MAY BE GETTING OLD

The solution to your worries is not to worry.

A woman I knew named Wendy recommended a daily 15 minute slot of worry time/ Her sister, Joan, wrote down her worries on scraps of paper and kept them in a mini-crate of colored popsicle sticks. She called it her "God Box."

They both smoked a lot of crack and grew prematurely wrinkled.

The only friend I ever had said *Watch the closing doors* every time
we entered an elevator or subway car. Once, she tripped over some guy's feet in a movie theater and sank straight down.

Are you all right? the gentleman inquired.

I've been on my knees before, she replied, gathering up her wooden mules
and pill vials.

Valium? She politely offered, as we took our seats.

Don't mind if I do, I responded, pulling two small bottles of Miller from my pocket.

We knew how to watch a flick back then.

I am the real deal.
I am a pillar of the downtown scene.
Young men told me that.
Everyone else ignores me.

30 years ago,
I sat on blankets selling books on Astor Place.
Jerry the Peddler tried to organize us but we were too busy
racing down the avenue, buying junk and selling works.
Blue tips were an investment.

All that authenticity streams though vessels and slows my legs.
All that authenticity is getting old and so are my peaches.
And pears.

I try to explain it without coffee.

I think I begin, *Don't think*, he interrupts
How do you not think? I wonder.
It's easy. You just accept, from moment to moment, then you don't have to think. You get in trouble when you think.
You worry when you worry.
You get in trouble when you think.
All that authenticity.
It's getting.
Old.

Melissa Gordon

A WEEK OF FAIRY TALES

Most nights you beg me
to tell you a story. I'm
afraid you can hear.

Night 1:
Evil queen. Snow.
White the fairest of them all?
Intolerable.

Night 2:
Enslaved by envy.
Pumpkin of beauty kindness.
Slipper's frail fortune.

Night 3:
Lifting the bell jar
found love behind a scared mask
broke. Kissed the rose spell.

Night 4:
Twisting jealousy.
Pixie dust can make you fly.
A hook's tender pain.

Night 5:
Did you ever see
in fairytales certain themes?
#1. Can evil please win.

I should be more fair:
#2. Incessant need for happily
(please) ever after.

Night 6:
#3. Honey, be happy.
If you prick your finger #4. some
day my prince will come.

Night 7:
She whined pined and cried.
Would you give up your voice for legs?
Be something you're not.

Where is that damn lamp?
#5. We shouldn't be left alone
to make wishes true.

Prissy lady with
scoundrel tramp? All twirling
spaghetti smooches.

You've stopped begging for a story. #6. I think you knew it was mine--soon yours.

Meghan Smith

FOR NOW

My daughter likes to carry things,
sometimes in her plump fingers
sometimes in an empty gift bag.
These things grant her safe conveyance,

for she cannot leave the house without
a wooden puzzle piece, mint floss, and
a small, red plastic ball that she nestles
in one sticky palm drawn up to her chest.

Right now, these things she carries
define themselves so openly
and provide easy remedy
to worry so exquisitely visible.

The lopsided button eyes on the green floral bear
plucked from the farmer's market stand
and tucked beneath her dimply elbow wing
reveal themselves an easy choking threat

and I cannot ignore the javelin point,
the imminence of impalement, on
the stick that she has rummaged from the bushes,
trailing tiny culverts behind her.

It takes little strategy to simply
uproot the bear from her crib,
to widen the distance between
its overlarge buttons and the smallness of her throat,

and she accepts the quick trade of her stick
for the wooden clack of the lawnmower
with alligators mouths that move,
pretending to eat up the green of the grass.

I don't want to think about
some of things she'll have to carry
when her hands have outgrown
the sticky curve of the little red ball.

These things will be too big to fit
inside a crumpled, pink gift bag,
too vast to tumble out the backside
of the alligator mower's jaws.

These things, which cannot be deemed
choking hazards or impalement risks,
will hide just behind the downward turn of her glossy lip
or lie along the waxed slant of her brows.

She will clutch them to her chest,
enclose them in the dark pink folds of her heart,
and pray my eyes were closed
to the places that she stashed them.

I will have to scheme and plan
grope the blurred boundaries of subtlety
to suggest she let me put them
out of her reach for awhile.

But, right now, I can still carry her,
scoop her into shade when the sun
has climbed too high in the sky.
I can coat her limbs in sunscreen

because I still believe that this disappearing lotion
that I have pulled from the pocket of my bag
will protect the newness of her skin,
seal in safety from the needle-pointed rays.

Claudia Van Gerven

SECRET ROOMS
After Bonnard's "Woman Undressing"

Marthe again, same small space
same pendulous breasts, hair
boyish drape of bangs

and dark thatch of the crotch
Her garb carelessly
tossed on the bed, for his

exquisite rendering—froth
on froth of nebulous whites—
hat red plumed or flowered

the pebbly-beige boots
with the jaunty heels
in the slight hold of

his anteroom. She is
cornered by the bed and twine-
seat chair with its quaint

shadows, the last leg hemmed
in the snare of her slip
And behind her, the mirror

that does not mirror her
but another room, one she
does not face, its reflection

a slice of elsewhere—what she
is not, what he will not—
mirroring their otherness

Alice B. Fogel

THE BEDROOM

Isn't it enough more than enough for you simply to live in the house simply
to be   awake in it to it again this morning to know it
exists around you newly sprung with light or rain   you know the house
watches over you   more than enough
that you never have to knock to be let in   for you are all
the doors to the house   admits you and just enough
of the sound of wind   chimes in the eaves outside your bedroom
soothe you   made your bed and laid in it lifted the covers
slid your legs linked in the fresh expanse of clean   percale beside yourself
every corner and alcove   yields without a reason
to importune   you know the answer
is yes   make up
your minds you do not need any more   to sleep
on it   is enough

Autumn Stephens

ELDERLY PRIMA GRAVIDA

History of a Girl
A blue cloud aureoles her hair, making her a madonna or hinting at the moment a smidge past perfection when petals begin their downward drift.

Labor Day
Without the children, she is left with too much fruit. Three platters on the drainboard, their chips and cracks mitigated by heaps of peaches, nectarines, plums. The sweet stones she dreamed of all winter, like Demeter, like her own mother, mourning loss of fragrance, sipping boiling water for comfort, reaching back toward a hotter life.

Spoiler
In the movie the children die. She should have chosen a different show, some summer trifle where the men are sex fools and the women are goddesses, sassy but forgiving. All the mistakes she's made, all the dangerous omissions. That afternoon when she and her friend sat griping pleasurably on the park bench: how did it happen that they commanded sunscreen, water bottles, yet still fell short, failed to precaution the two boys, the girl, against every danger? Failed to extend the protective mantle of maternal instruction against stray dogs, strange men, slippery banks, polluted water, so on. Failed to say, quite explicitly, that it was forbidden to hike up to the waterfall. But then, they were old mothers, decades fanning out behind them as they imagined their children into life. They had gotten away with murder, redefined the status quo. At what point would exceptions no longer be made? At what point would there no longer be time?

Fruitless
For sex he wakes her, laying a hand on some round part. It's too early—she's set the alarm for a hundred years. "Go away, I'm practicing," she says. Curved forms appear lenient but she's not. No one's worn a white petticoat since maybe 1969. Under sweatshirt and mom jeans, her spotted skin, her graying hair.

Nancy Vona

KAREN AT THE SENIOR PROM, 1985

Body sheathed in strapless blue satin
she sways with her partner.

We hate her midnight hair
her periwinkle eyes
the smugness of her arrogance.

She is a Helen in our small town
We check the stalls
in the faux marble bathroom

and exclaim in whispers! Over her flat stomach!
Who is the baby's father?
Did she really give *it* up?

If she hears the gossip,
she doesn't react.
Our words float to the gilded ceiling
and collect dust and jealousy.

She has been to a cool bed of ferns
known a sunrise in her body
heard the mourning dove's cry

the cry we virgins
are afraid to understand.

Susan Vespoli

GUAM 1973

Where apples are shaped like stars
and beef shipped from Australia tastes green.
Where eggrolls are lumpia rolled by men in purple bell-bottoms.
Where teriyaki meat is grilled above fire
and fondue pots melt cheese
and sticky red rice forms moist domes on fiesta plates.

Where Janis Joplin wails in a cave
on a gray day along Tarague Beach
where the coral reef is pink
where pot smoke and 8-track tunes fill Datsuns
and the ramada jukebox plays "All Right Now."
Where rattan wears floral cushions
and geckos fleck shower walls in base housing
and German Shepherds walk with guards after dark.

Where your mother stirs Instant Breakfast into milk,
Hurry you'll miss the bus.
Where the bus driver's eye-whites flash red
and his teeth are darkened by betel-nut
and lunch ladies turn peanut-buttered bread into shiny, flat squares
and milk tastes oddly sweet and lying in the sun is a sport.

Where the bomb threats are constant, though the war is almost over
and the overflow of GIs camp in tents
and the Skyview shows movies where we lie on the grass
and our feet are always bare and our bras have been burned
and the birth control clinic is a room downtown where girls give fake names and birthdates
and wait months for appointments while their bellies swell
and adoptions are arranged until abortions become legal
and tall, dumb boys hand you capsules to start your period
and your school counselor says most girls don't finish high school
and your mom looks away and starts golf lessons
and your dad smiles after bomb drops
and the guy brings up marriage

and your sister asks, *What do you think you are? A science project?*
and you tell everyone to fuck off
because one day the baby will turn forty
and still be one of the best things that ever happened to you.

Margaret Rozga

MY SHADOW IS A SILENT MOVIE

dark and graceful as Chaplin's Little Tramp
but faceless.

My face is a shadow of my mother's.
My sisters and brother favor my dad.

Returning a favor is both the shadow
and substance of gratitude.

Women who hunger for substantial words
emerge from the shadows.

Hunger is a powerful shadow.
Shade is the shadow of color.

Orange colors the monarch
calls forth unshadowed awe.

The owl's call questions dawn,
sometimes overshadows light.

Imitation is sometimes
the sincerest form of shadowing.

Shadowing those women who hunger
for and learn the magic of face to face,

I face the danger of caring.
I cast spells of my own.

Alina Borger

HOUSE FINCH LUNES

red head, red
streaked tail, red breast, fleckled
back and wings

perches, preens, pretends
not to see through our
glass patio door.

David references Sibley's
Guide to Birds, careful precision
turns pages, scanning—

the Purple Finch
candidate lives too far west,
wears darker hues,

fascinates us less
than our more common guests,
the House Finches.

Hopping then swooping
between our railings, ready to
find, to mate.

Our son wonders
What are they fighting over?
And we explain

It's not fighting.
Our bemused memories of yesterday
intrude. We blush,

clean up breakfast
touch each other's backs, squeeze
hands, get dressed.

LaToya Jordan

LOVE, AGAIN

We are favorite blue jeans
spun long in the dryer on hot.

Jiggle our limbs into tight
waistlines. Suck it in, squat.

We keep wearing each other,
stretch, until the fit is easy.

Louisa Howerow

ADVICE GIVEN AT THE MARKET

The produce man calls me over,
says I might like something hot
this weekend to pair with bland
and boiled, something like what
he holds in his hand, a habanero
wrinkled, chocolate brown
to drop in whole or cleave open
this here's no seasoning pepper
this here's zinger and burn,
guaranteed to fire up your pot,
ward off evil spirits, and if
I want to swing it sweet,
well then *this here habanero's*
all game. I'm to blend it with mango,
with papaya, inhale the fragrance,
check back with him next Saturday.

Carol Dorf

CURVILINEAR SPACE (ARTIST'S STATEMENT VERSION 22)

It seemed easy when I first started dealing with the lack
of corners in my room -- ok why settle for the tyranny
of the right angle, bookshelves can form a room divider
if it comes to that. The problem was meeting myself
coming and going; and the way my children never met
a barrier and wouldn't stop running in circles, then laughing
uproariously each time they crashed into me. I took
to wearing padded coats and pants like a peasant. Back
against the wall lost meaning. White walls stopped
being a refuge, and I started using more colors in my work.

Jennifer Schomburg Kanke

PRAYER OF MY LABORING MOTHER

Let us make it to the city
so that the first sounds she hears
may be the beeping of machines,
the soft padding of sensible
leather shoes on linoleum.
Keep the creek in the culvert,
and the baying of the hound,
keep the cicadas cry,
and spring peepers, keep them
across the county line.
Let them snip the webbing
from between her two long toes,
let concrete be her friend.

Katrinka Moore

GRAVITY

Dozes as they drive, the boy asleep on her lap. Her husband thinks of the future, their son dreams of the ocean. Here is where she lives. Alone she would walk to the shadowy mountains, touch them.

Swallowed by elements. Something open, dust, air.

A rare creek, juncos, finches, cottonwood tree. Wade, splash, laugh, lie on the bank to dry.

Her mother left behind, the river. A thousand miles of dusty road. If they meet another car, they stop, trade stories.

Bodies in motion, inertia. A crow blocks the way, eating carrion. They pull around, crushing a prickly pear. She knows to throw spilled salt, to knock on wood, but what to do about passing a crow? Empty space left ajar, sliver in the margins.

Faith Williams

RIDING THE DREAMS (1977)

all of us   the women of my town
like a company of witches
rising out of our houses
in the middle of the night
patting gently our husbands stretched out in pajamas
tenderly kissing our children goodbye
savoring their sweet milky smell
waving and going out past the rows of dark houses
We brush back our graying hair
and hold hands together
We look forward and see
the length of the field, a long valley
settled with siloes and barns
Beyond lie the blue mountains
and over them, who knows?

Sally Deskins, "Magical Garden"

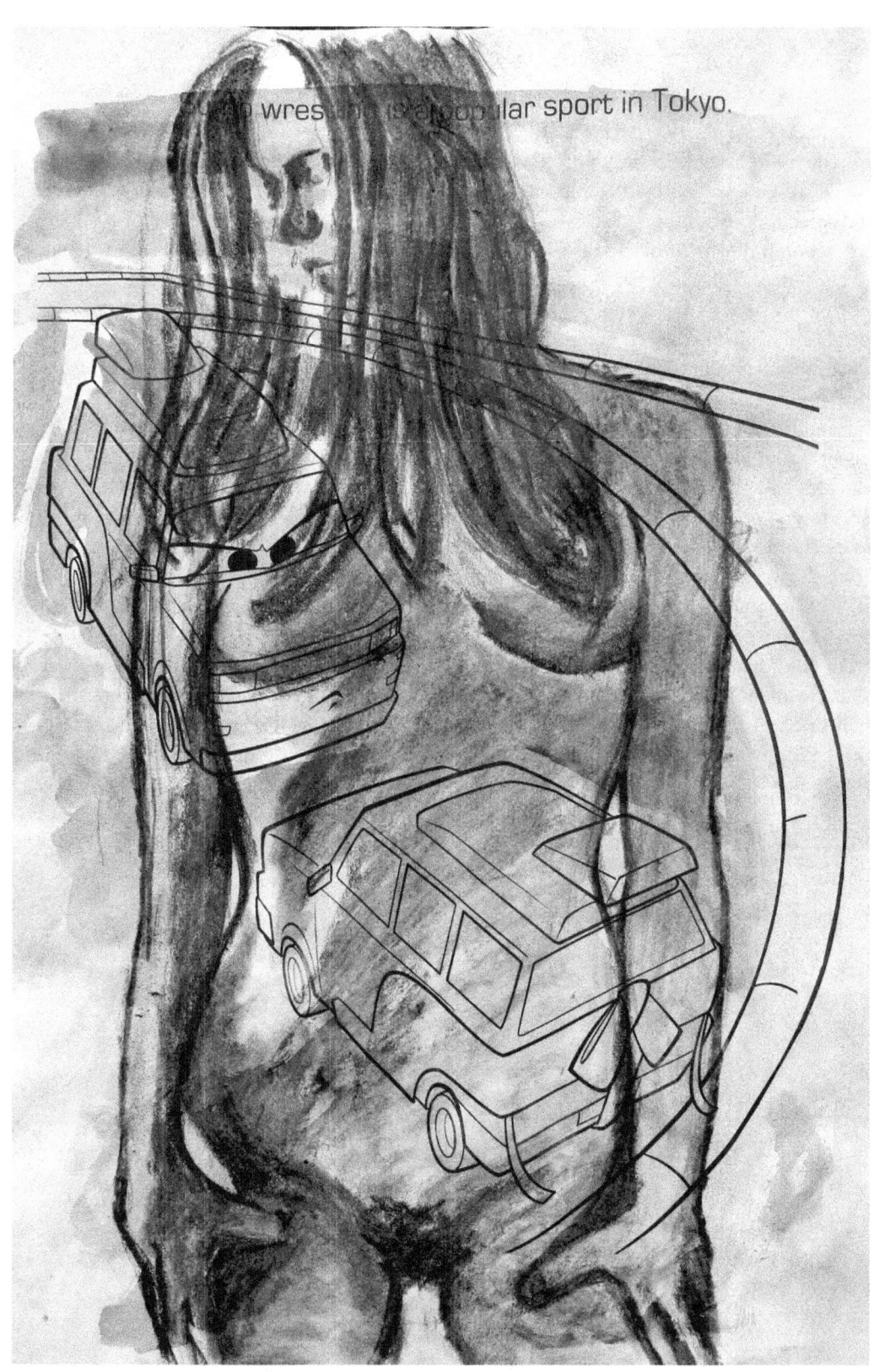

Sally Deskins, "Sport Mixed USA"

Radhiyah Ayobami

my son and i have developed a little routine...when he goes to basketball practice, i go to a cafe nearby to read and write...he often gets annoyed with me because i watch to make sure he's safely in the building...today he said, you don't have to watch me, i'm tired of that! and stomped off down the block, fussing about missing happy hour at taco bell with his friends (when some of that junky 'food' is half-price) i called him back to me and told him that having a conscious and loving pair of eyes watching for him was far better than any taco bell...i told him how much i missed my grandmother and my father's eyes looking out for me with the wisdom of their years and the strength of their love protecting and guiding me, and how much more i appreciate my mother, who is sharp-eyed and steady, watching for both me and him...i told him how many people go through life without a parent or a protector or anyone with kind eyes watching for them, and how impossible it is for one person to see all the hills and gullies on the path ahead, how useful it is to have a trusted guide to see and be able to say- watch out! did you try this? how bout that?...my grandmother often told me a story about when i was three or so, skipping and playing far ahead of her, when a man came from the doorway of a building and started to follow me...i never saw this man, but my 5 ft, 130 lb grandmother threw down her cigarette and told him, man if you lay one hand on that child, we both going to meet our maker today! i told him that is the lineage we come from- and that i will watch for him while i'm on this earth plane and beyond- because that's the agreement i made with the universe when i became a mother- and ain't that better than a half-price taco? after all that he couldn't do nothing but gimme my hug and go on his way- but he did wave to me as he went into the building and i stood on the corner watching- and that makes me think he understands

Lindsey Bellosa

MORE THAN HOME

"To lose the earth you know for greater knowing; to lose the life you have for greater life; to leave the friends you have loved, for greater loving; to find a land more kind than home, more large than Earth" – Thomas Wolfe.

"Stay with me; the world is dark and wild."-The Witch, Into the Woods.

It is human nature to strike out—
to know the unknowable; to put new names
on wild places; to find out who else may be

in the forest of the world. Home is a small place,
with ordinary trappings; our table is not enough
when the world is so large.

For this reason, I dress and put on lipstick and kiss
you and your brother good night. You ask me
to bring you back a watermelon.

Someday, little son, you will sail out into the large world
with the four-fingered stars of your storybooks behind you,
having decided home has nothing you don't already know.

But what is there greater to know than love, and love
has been yours since you filled my arms? And yet,
we search for more. Our blood is always rushing, wild

and dark. The stars are ringing in such a vast sky
of possibilities. I will bring you back watermelon,
round as the earth. I will bring back fruitless hope

that you will know the unknowable:
that the stories are true as long as you believe them.
Nothing is sweeter than what you've already tasted.

Lynne Shapiro

WHAT GOOD WAS/ IS

The children shaped
small pieces of wool
          found inside socks, shoes & pockets
into felt horses, houses & hats

They placed the leftover bits
on the highest branches
          they could reach
for the song birds' arrival.

Grace Mattern

RITUAL

Music summons the wise
daemon, notes of young genius
stirring. We light candles
with wishes, untether

the expectations of smoke.
A chorus of voices rises
above the scotch and red wine
and we remember exactly

what we meant when we said
exquisite. Time has been kind,
we try not to repeat last year's
desires. No one cries, none of us

died, our circle gathered again;
the sun creaks, stops, reverses.

Charlotte Mandel

COSMOLOGY OF THE HUMAN

Astronomers agree the universe
enacts a kind of suicide
by burning.
The urns of imploded stars
accelerate in space while new suns
jar the constellations.

In time, the compact
sack in which one lives
bristles in friction—the body
drills the way
an embryo forces gills, wing-
stubs, thumbs, heart launching
electric charge
the blood ferries safely
on its salt

to sound of
words distantly booming,
inland sea stirring our breaths,
tears letting us know
how close we come
every second of a life
to drowning.

We cling for safety to the palms
of our own hands, the chafe

of friable skin
whining narrow and sharp until

spark ignites
bluewhite fires long gone
into whirlpools, old stars
making room.

Lori Lamothe

HOUSE OF USHER

It still surprises you, that the hand
rising from depths of mirror
            never surfaces.
Year after year, you go on
sailing across the lake of happiness,
the light sparking on ordinary fears,
reality a smooth glass
painted with clouds crossing silver.
                    How many days
have you traced a fingertip over time
and watched its circles rippling?

True, there are moments when the images—
the child, the house, the dog
sprawled asleep before the fire—waver,
the reflections threatening to dissolve
into a lifetime of bad luck.
And sometimes, late at night,
            when the moon
loses itself behind shadow,
you feel yourself floating along empty hallways.
You know then what you always wanted—
the plunge through darkness, the swimming
toward the lost twin, the one true self.

Fay Chiang

FOUR SHORT POEMS

I. The Heat Scorches

The heat scorches
        us
    like bleached bones
    on desert floor
        turned to dust
    and blown to the winds

the rains will come
the rains will come
yes, the rains will come

II. Your Eyes

Your eyes
    are warm, brown, fluid
  I see my self
        in them

III. Sakura Blossoms

Sakura blossoms
    have fallen
        we have missed
            the bloom and
    our frenzied lives
        wasted moments

  I must journey on---
        Mount Fuji calls

IV. At 63

At 63
  mind clear
  heart calm
  soul ever restless

Let's see what remains
    in the landscape
        of this life
    when the past stills for now
        the present shimmers
            and the future opens
                fearlessly

Cheryl Byler Keeler

MAMMOGRAM

Glad to see me again? says the technician
at my six-month diagnostic. She raises
her eyebrows to be clear—I'm lucky
to be pinched, pressed and flattened,
to talk about how school starts soon, how
the memory goes after forty, how
her husband thinks touching breasts
all day is a job to die for. *They're just
tissue with nipples*, she tells him. *Men!* she
tells me raising eyebrows again. It is clear. I am
lucky to be pinched, pressed and flattened
two years since the carnivorous lump.
When she returns to report *looks good!* relief
ripples like high tide in all my tissues.
I raise my eyebrows—*to tissue
with nipples!* I tell her.

Emily Spencer

THIS IS HOW I WANT TO LIVE MY LIFE

The man I dated two months ago is finger painted on my walls,
running, by my five-year-old daughter who is a cave person,
lately. *Is it okay to raise a bat?*

Her stuffed animals are more
real and civilized—Mr. White Lion, Mrs. African Tiger—
than myself and the running men. She paints in a timeline
while I mark our heights in every doorframe. *See, Mother,*
you are not growing.

My daughter is finger painting then playing with dead ants,
getting stung by a bee, or scattering the flies. I will not push her.

I will not push the wine boxes away from the door until
we go buy food. The local people stare across the checkouts
at our hair done in semidarkness and wonder what happened
to me. Might I take the salmon out
holding it with my teeth
like mama bears splashing in the Tuolumne River.
They kill hikers and they kill juvenile salmon—blood
of offspring, red rapids.

I tell my big-eyed child
to splash water on her hair in the bathroom.
Yes, Mother.

My child comes out wet.
I am a fish. I am silverfish.

In September, she will go to school and I will stop living how I want
to live my life. The house will be emptied of flies, bees, dead ants for pink
tea cookies and a schoolgoing party. She might never have to answer, "Why
do you live your life this way?

Don't you want to live your life?"

Sarah Sadie

THE WORLD TREE GROWS AT WESTGATE MALL

Parked in front of Hancock Fabrics waiting,
hazards blinking, for my son to emerge
from choir rehearsal this raw March evening,
I sit in an acre or more of early thaw
and broken, rutted pavement, dingy cars,
trees still bare. Yellowed, sickly lights
and neon signs falter in deepening blue.
A radio tower blinks dark then red then dark.
I keep the car's engine running for the heat.

Reflected in the shallow still of a puddle,
a piece of tree. It catches me, I look up
and down, from copy to original
and back again. It's just
one anonymous young tree plunked down
in a row in a parking strip. But the small segment
caught in water and mirrored in every twig
becomes something else again, as dusk deepens,
becomes possibility.

I do not understand these chemistries,
why reflections hold us, or how a fragment
keens and catches more than its whole.
I only know how restful it is to gaze
at this puddle, the shard of tree reflected, how
I look long and long as cars splash through, each time
scattering the surface with dirty, crud-crusted tires,
and each time, each time, the water restores itself.

Karen Craigo

BREAKING THE SHELL OF THE YEAR

The new year
cracks open
like an egg,
and the neighbor
has stopped by
with a bowl
of hoppin' John—
small offering
of sustenance
and good fortune.
I know a farmer
who sells double-yolks,
but each one
is still a small surprise,
like two suns occupying
the same stretch of sky.
Maybe this year
will bring surprises,
and at the end
of a revolution
I'll be famous.
The paparazzi
won't let me be,
because no one
can get enough
of the life of a poet,
or maybe because
I carry my own camera,
and here is what I look like
as I lean into the couch pillow,
one hand over my eyes
while I reach
to find another word
for "new."
This novel year
I shall try to remain
humble as I
commit myself
to finding what light
a scramble of words
can offer.

CONTRIBUTORS

Olga Abella's poems have appeared in *black dirt, CALYX, Urban Spaghetti, Natural Bridge, The MacGuffin, poetrybay.com, poetpourri, Long Island Quarterly, Ginosko, Kalliope, Red Ochre, Main Street Rag, Verse Wisconsin*; and in two chapbooks, *Grasping to What Is* (A Short Book Press 1993) and *What It Takes* (Birnham Wood Graphics 2000), and a book, *Watching the Wind* (Writers Ink Press 2008).

Kristin Agudelo's poems have been published in a number of online and in-print journals, including *The Commonline Journal, Fear of Monkeys, The Cafe Review,* and *Literary Mama.* When not writing poetry, she single-parents her nine-year-old son, teaches Humanities at a Waldorf high school in Maine, and maintains a blog on women's history and literature at www.notablewomen.wordpress.com.

Nina R. Alonso's poems have appeared in *The New Yorker, Ploughshares, Ibbetson Street, Sumac, U. Mass. Review, WomenPoems, Bagel Bards, New Boston Review, Muddy River Poetry Review,* etc., and her book *This Body* was published by David Godine Press. Her stories, including a Pushcart nominee, were in *Southern Women's Review* and, most recently, *Broadkill Review.*

E.J. Antonio is a 2009 fellow in Poetry from the New York Foundation for the Arts and a recipient of fellowships from the Hurston/Wright Foundation and the Cave Canem Foundation. She is the author of two chapbooks, *Every Child Knows*; Premier Poets Chapbook Series 2007, *Solstice*, Red Glass Books, 2013. Her debut CD, *Rituals in the marrow: Recipe for a jam session* was released in the fall of 2010. www.ejantoniobluez.net.

Radhiyah Ayobami-- Brooklyn-born by way of the south, telling stories of black womanhood, motherhood & folks in invisible spaces, believes word has the power to shift consciousness, writes & workshops with pregnant teens, inmates & elders, Africana Studies graduate of Brooklyn College & MFA Prose student at Mills College in Oakland, California, where she is working on a collection of nonfiction essays & the trees give her poems.

Jessie Bacho is a NJ writer and English adjunct at several local colleges. In her spare time, she enjoys recreating scenes from The Muppet Show with her two sons. Her work has appeared in Germ Magazine, The Legendary, Ars Poetica, In Other Words..., and Prism. Please visit her website www.jessiebacho.com or follow her on Twitter @ jessiebacho.

Janet Barry is a New Hampshire musician and poet with works in numerous journals and anthologies, most recently *Trickster, Two Hawks Quarterly, Edge, Prairie Wolf Press* and *The Fourth River.* She serves yearly as a judge for Poetry-Out-Loud, and has received numerous Pushcart, Best of the Net, and BiLine nominations. Janet holds degrees in organ performance and poetry.

Christine Beck holds an M F A from Southern Connecticut State University. She is the author of *Blinding Light* (Grayson Books 2014). Her poems have been published in *Connecticut Review, Passager,* and *Connecticut River Review. The Charlotte Chronicles* won a mini-chapbook award from The Centrifugal Eye in 2013. Her chapbook, *Flying with the Man Who Looks at Not*hing is forthcoming in 2015 from Dancing Girl Press. She teaches poetry, creative writing and literature. Her website is http://ChristineBeck.net.

Lindsey Bellosa lives in Syracuse, NY. She has an MA in Writing from the National University of Ireland, Galway and has poems published in both Irish and American journals: most recently *The Comstock Review, The Galway Review, IthacaLit, Crannog* and *The MOON Magazine.* Her first chapbook, *The Hunger*, was published with Willet Press in 2014.

Susie Berg is the co-curator of Toronto's Plasticine Poetry Reading Series. Her work appears in her poetry collection, *How to Get Over Yourself,* her blog, The Starbucks Poetry Project, and several periodicals and anthologies. She has two chapbooks forthcoming in 2015. Visit her online at www.sber40.wix.com/susieberg, or follow her @SusieDBerg on Twitter.

Deborah L. Blicher is a Boston-area essayist, editor, and coach. Her work has appeared in *Brain, Child; Lilith;* and *The Boston Globe Magazine.* Her website (always in progress) is www.deborahblicher.org.

Emily R. Blumenfeld is a writing facilitator in the area of the therapeutic and transformative uses of language. She is the author of three illustrated booklets, *Liquid Words; Love and Dust: Notes from the Kitchen Floor*, and *The Shelter of Our Words* (Prehensile Pencil Publications/The Feral Press).

Emma Bolden is the author of *Maleficae* (GenPop Books, 2013) and *medi(t)ations*, forthcoming from Noctuary Press. She's also the author of four chapbooks of poetry -- *How to Recognize a Lady* (Toadlily Press); *The Mariner's Wife* (Finishing Line Press); *The Sad Epistles* (Dancing Girl Press); *This Is Our Hollywood* (The Chapbook) – and one nonfiction chapbook – *Geography V* (Winged City Press).

Born outside Boston, **Zachary Bond** now splits his time between Boston and Poughkeepsie, NY where he recently completed his Film Production degree at Vassar. In 2014, his short documentary, "The Seer of Poughkeepsie" saw press on the *Huffington Post Blog* and he received the Beatrice Daw Brown Prize for Poetry. His work has appeared in *Black Heart Magazine*.

Alina Borger is a writer and a high-school teacher in Iowa City, IA. Most recently, her work has been published in *Brain, Child* and *Kindred*. When she's not writing or teaching, she's cheering for light-saber wars between her two boys or curling up with a book and a mug of chamomile tea. Find her on Twitter @AliBG.

Beth Bosworth is the author most recently of *The Source of Life and Other Stories* (University of Pittsburgh Press, 2012 Drue Heinz Literature Prize). Her other books are *A Burden of Earth and Other Stories* (Hanging Loose Press), and the novel *Tunneling* (Crown Publishers). Her work has appeared in *The Kenyon Review, AGNI, Guernica, The Seneca Review* and elsewhere. Bosworth is founding editor of *The Saint Ann's Review* and lives in Brooklyn with her family.

Rosalie Calabrese is a native New Yorker and a management consultant for the arts who writes poetry, short stories and librettos for musicals. Her poems have appeared in publications ranging from *And Then* to *Cosmopolitan, Jewish Currents* to *Poetry New Zealand*, plus in newspapers, anthologies, and on line. Her chapbook *Remembering Chris* is published by Poets Wear Prada.

Jennifer Campbell is an English professor in Buffalo, NY, and a co-editor of Earth's Daughters. Her second book of poetry, *Supposed to Love*, was published by Saddle Road Press in 2013. Recent work appears in *Saranac Review, Comstock Review, The Prompt, Oyez Review, Common Ground Review, Sow's Ear, Fugue,* and *The Healing Muse*, and is forthcoming in *Seems*. www.jennifer-campbell.com.

Wendy Taylor Carlisle is the author of two books, *Reading Berryman to the Dog* and *Discount Fireworks* (Jacaranda Books) and three chapbooks, the most recent of which is *Persephone on the Metro*, (Mad Hat Books, 2014.) See her work at www.wendytaylorcarlisle.com

Fay Chiang is a poet and visual artist who believes culture is a spiritual and psychological weapon used for the empowerment of people and communities. Working at Project Reach (www.projectreachnyc.org), a center for young people at risk in Chinatown/Lower East Side, she is also a member of Zero Capital and the Orchard Street Advocacy and Wellness Center. Battling her 8th bout of breast cancer, she is working on her memoir. *Seven Continents Nine Lives* (Bowery Books) is her most recent collection of poetry. And she is the mother of the inimitable Xian.

Patrice Boyer Claeys holds a Certificate in Poetry from the Writer's Studio at the University of Chicago. She has taught workshops for the Northwest Cultural Council and last year received Honorable Mention in their annual poetry contest. Her work has appeared in the *Mom Egg Review, Found Poetry Review, Blue Heron Review, The Avocet, ARDOR,* and the *NWCC 2012 Poet and Artist Chapbook*.

Queer poet **Louie Clay** (né Louie Crew), 77, is an Alabama native and an emeritus professor at Rutgers. He lives in East Orange, NJ, with Ernest 'Cut' Clay, his husband of 40 years. Louie Clay is the founder of Integrity, an activist ministry of LGBTQ Episcopalians/Anglicans. In addition to his Ph.D. he holds honorary doctorates from three seminaries of The Episcopal Church. Editors have published 2,324 of Louie Clay's poems and essays. The University of Michigan collects Clay's papers. You can follow his work at http://rci.rutgers.edu/~lcrew/pubs.html.

Marion Deutsche Cohen's latest poetry book is *Lights I Have Loved*. Her books total 23 -- not including, as of this week, a forthcoming poetry collection, *Closer to Dying* but yes-including two memoirs: *Still the End: Memoir of a Nursing Home Wife*, and its prequel *Dirty Details: The Days and Nights of a Well Spouse*. She teaches math and writing at Arcadia University in Glenside PA, where she has developed the course, Truth and Beauty: Mathematics in Literature. Also, Marion has a poem in a previous issue of *Mom Egg Review*.

Karen Craigo teaches English to international students at Drury University in Springfield, Missouri. A chapbook, *Someone Could Build Something Here*, was published by Winged City Chapbook Press in 2013, and her previous chapbook, *Stone for an Eye*, is part of the Wick Poetry Series. Her work has appeared in the journals *Atticus Review, Poetry, Indiana Review, Prairie Schooner, Puerto del Sol, The MacGuffin,* and others. Her blog, *Better View of the Moon*, is at betterviewofthemoon.blogspot.com.

Edward D. Currelley is an author and artist. He was awarded honorable status in 2008 by Writers Digest for Stage Playwriting. His children's book *I'm Not Lost, I'm With You* will be published in 2015. He is the president of Pen To Mind Books & Child Development Concepts, Inc. He resides in New York City.

Lorraine Currelley is a poet, writer, Mental Health Counselor and member of the Pearls of Wisdom Storytellers and is the Founder/Executive Director of Poets Network & Exchange, Inc. She is published widely and has performed her work extensively. She resides in New York City.

Shannon J. Curtin is a 2014 Pushcart Prize nominee and the author of two collections of poetry, *Motherland* (forthcoming from Anchor & Plume Press), and *File Cabinet Heart* (ELJ Publications, 2014), Her poetry has been featured in a variety of literary magazines including *Short, Fast, and Deadly, The Muddy River Review, Vox Poetica,* and *The Camel Saloon*. She holds an MBA, competitive shooting records, and her liquor. She would probably like you.

Kimberly Dark is a writer, professor, parent and performer. She tells stories about the body in culture - how the contours of privilege and oppression influence our daily lives. She is the author of five award-winning performance scripts and her stories, poems and essays appear in numerous academic and trade publications. She teaches in a graduate program in Sociological Practice at Cal State San Marcos. Learn more at www.kimberlydark.com.

Holly Day lives in Minneapolis, Minnesota, where she teaches writing classes at the Loft Literary Center. Her recently-published books include *Music Theory for Dummies, Piano All-in-One for Dummies*, and *A Brief History of Nordeast Minneapolis*.

Sarah J. Den Boer's chapbook *Sawdust, Sugarcube* was published in 2009 by dancing girl press. She was a Stegner Fellow at Stanford University from 2010-2012. She lives in Edmonton, Alberta, with her husband and daughter, and works at an inner city homeless shelter.

Sally Deskins is an artist and writer. Her artwork has been exhibited nationally and writing published in *Stirring, Bookslut* and *Bitch* among others. She is founding editor of *Les Femmes Folles: Women in Art*, and illustrated *Intimates and Fools* (poetry by Laura Madeline Wiseman, Les Femmes Folles Books, 2014). Sallydeskins.tumblr.com.

Chelsea Dingman was raised in the Rockies of British Columbia, and later in Edmonton, Canada. She currently lives in south Florida. Her work has been published in *RHINO Poetry Journal* (forthcoming), *Yemassee* (forthcoming), *OVS, Stone Highway Review, Slipstream,* and *Vermillion Literary Project*, among others. She continues her MFA this fall.

Carol Dorf's poetry has been published in *Mom Egg Review, Spillway, Sin Fronteras, Antiphon, Composite, About Place, The Journal of Humanistic Mathematics, Scientific American, Maintenant, OVS Best of Indie Lit New England,* and elsewhere. She is poetry editor of *Talking Writing* and teaches mathematics at Berkeley High School. Website: http://talkingwriting.com/.

Melissa Eleftherion grew up in Brooklyn. She is the author of *huminsect* (dancing girl press, 2013), *prism maps* (dusie kollektiv, 2014), *Pigtail Duty* (forthcoming in 2015 from dancing girl press), and several other chapbooks and fragments. She works as a librarian with Mendocino County Libraries, and created, developed, and currently manages the Poetry Center Chapbook Exchange. apoetlibrarian.wordpress.com.

Beverly Butler Faragasso notes that because several illnesses have affected her family, she often writes about the challenges that caregivers and their loved ones face. Her essay, "The Street," won first prize for non-fiction in the 2014 Writers' Circle, Inc. contest. It recreates one frightening day when her husband, who has Parkinson's, had difficulty walking.

Alice B. Fogel is New Hampshire's poet laureate. She is the author of several books of poems and a "how-to" called *Strange Terrain*, on appreciating poetry without necessarily "getting" it. Nominated 7 times for the Pushcart, she has received a fellowship from the National Endowment for the Arts and other awards. Her newest book, *Interval: Poems Based on Bach's "Goldberg Variations"* is out April 2015.

Laura Foley is the author of four poetry collections. *Joy Street*, was released in 2014. *The Glass Tree* won the ForeWord Book of the Year Award in Poetry (Silver) and was a Finalist for the New Hampshire Writer's Project, Outstanding Book of Poetry. She lives on a woody hill in Vermont with her partner and their three big dogs. laurafoley.net.

Jennifer L. Freed writes mostly poetry and occasionally some short fiction. Her work has appeared in lit-mags such as *The Atlanta Review, Poetry East, The Common Ground Review* and *Literary Mama*, and in the medical journals *CHEST* and *JAMA*. She was a finalist in the 2013 New Woman Voices chapbook contest for *These Hands Still Holding*. jfreed.weebly.com

Gail Ghai's poetry and reviews have appeared in *Descant, JAMA, Poet Works, Women's Review of Books* and the Yearbook of American Poetry. Awards include a Pushcart Prize nomination and a Henry C. Frick scholarship for creative teaching. She was a recent semi-finalist in the Mary Ballard Chapbook Competition.

Maria Mazziotti Gillan is a recipient of AWP's 2014 George Garrett Award, Poets & Writers' 2011 Barnes & Noble Writers for Writers Award, and the 2008 American Book Award. She is founder/executive director of the Poetry Center at Passaic County Community College, editor of the *Paterson Literary Review*, and director of creative writing/professor of English at Binghamton University-SUNY.

Melissa Gordon is currently an MFA student at Western Connecticut State University where she is editor of *Poor Yorick*, the program's online literary journal. Her poetry has been published in *DMQ Review* and is forthcoming in *Gyroscope Review*. She also works at Yale University conducting substance use research and is a contributing author on several articles in the *American Journal of Psychiatry*.

Atoosa Grey is a poet and singer/songwriter living in Brooklyn, NY. She holds an MFA in Creative Writing from The New School where she was an honoree for the Paul Violi Poetry Prize 2013. Her poems have previously appeared in *Right Hand Pointing, Fat City Review, Mandala Review, the Best American Poetry Blog*, and *Eunoia Review*.

Heather Haldeman lives in Pasadena, California. She has been married to her husband, Hank, for thirty-six years and has three grown children. Her work has been published in *The Christian Science Monitor, Chicken Soup for the Soul, From Freckles to Wrinkles, Grandmother Earth, Mom Egg Review*, and numerous online journals. She has received first, second and third prizes for her essays. Currently, she is working on a memoir about growing up in wealth and ruin in Los Angeles during the Mad Men era.

Jane Harrington has written books for young adults (Scholastic, Lerner) and is now crafting literary fiction and creative nonfiction in Virginia's Blue Ridge, where she lives, writes and teaches college writing. Her work has appeared in *Chautauqua, Mom Egg Review, Anthology of Appalachian Writers,* and *Portland Review*. She is a fellow at the Virginia Center for the Creative Arts.

Lois Marie Harrod's thirteenth and fourteenth poetry collections *Fragments from the Biography of Nemesis* (Cherry Grove Press) and the chapbook *How Marlene Mae Longs for Truth* (Dancing Girl Press) appeared in 2013. Her poems and stories have appeared in literary journals and online ezines from *American Poetry Review* to *Zone 3*. Read more work on www.loismarieharrod.org.

Jamie Lynn Heller has two young girls, the perfect spouse, a high school counseling career she loves, and she gets to write. She is a Pushcart Prize nominee and the author of *Domesticated, Poetry from Around the House*. Jamie has poetry published in *Prairie Schooner, Tule Review, Noctua Review, Little Balkans Review* and others. For a list of publications see jamielynnheller.blogspot.com.

Rage Hezekiah is a former farmer, baker, and doula currently pursuing her MFA at Emerson College. She was a Showcase Poet in the Fall 2014 issue of The Aurorean. Her poems have been anthologized in *Other Tongues: Mixed Race Women Speak Out*, and are forthcoming in *Glassworks* and *Freshwater*. Her work has also appeared in *Fifth Wednesday, Nepantla,* and other journals.

April Clark Honaker is an instructor of English at Louisiana Tech University where she teaches composition and technical writing. She received a 2012-13 Artist Career Advancement Grant from the Louisiana Division of the Arts. Her work has been published in *The 2River View* and in *Southern Voice,* an online literary publication of *Deep South Magazine.*

Louisa Howerow's latest poems appeared in *Antiphon, A Common Thread* and *The Nashwaak Review*. Her poetry has also been included in anthologies, most recently, *I Found It at the Movies: An Anthology of Film Poems* (Guernica Editions) and *Imaginarium 3: The Best Canadian Speculative Writing,* 2014 (ChiZine Publications).

Molly Howes's publications include the *New York Times* "Modern Love" column, *Boston Globe Magazine, Bellingham Review* and *Passages North*. The grateful recipient of fellowships from Ragdale and MacDowell, she otherwise lives in Massachusetts with her husband and any of their grown children they can corral. Her memoir, *The Temporary Orphan: A Tale of Invisible Wounds and Unexpected Grace*, is almost completed.

Vicki Iorio is a native Long Islander. You can find her work in various print and on line publications. *Poems from thevDirty Couch* is Iorio's first full-length poetry collection.

Jennifer Jean's most recent poetry collection is *The Fool*. Other collections include: *In the War, Fishwife,* and *The Archivist*. Her work has appeared in: *Drunken Boat, Denver Quarterly, Caketrain, Tidal Basin Review, Talking/Writing*, and more. She Co-directs the Morning Garden Artist Retreats, is Poetry Editor for The Compassion Project: An Anthology; and, she teach Free2Write poetry workshops for sex-trafficking survivors.

LaToya Jordan lives in Brooklyn, New York with her husband and preschooler. She received an MFA in Creative Writing from Antioch University Los Angeles. Her poetry has appeared in *Radius, Mobius: The Journal for Social Change, MiPoesias*, and more. Her chapbook, *Thick-Skinned Sugar*, is available now from Finishing Line Press. Visit her at latoyajordan.com.

Jennifer Schomburg Kanke is a doctoral candidate at Florida State University. Her work has appeared in *Prairie Schooner, Pleiades*, and *Court Green*. Her website can be found at www.jenniferschomburgkanke.com.

Donna Katzin is Executive Director of Shared Interest, a social investment fund supporting equitable development in Southern Africa, and a board member of the Center for Community Change. Proud mother of Sari and Daniel and wife of Alan, she is the author of *With These Hands – poems for the new South Africa* (available only from www.shared interest.org).

Cheryl Keeler writes that poems arrive, line by line, in her life. She is grateful when they do. Some have been shared in *5AM, The Dirty Napkin, International Psychoanalysis, Mom Egg Review, Hospital Drive* and *BODY.*

Hilary King is a poet and playwright living in Atlanta, Georgia. Her poems have appeared in *PANK, Gertrude, Stone Highway Review, Blue Fifth Review* and other publications. Her plays have been produced across the US and in Australia. More about Hilary, her family and her pup, Woozy, can be found at hilarykingwriter.com.

Sandra Kohler's third collection of poems, *Improbable Music*, appeared in May, 2011 from Word Press. Her two previous collections are *The Ceremonies of Longing*, winner of the 2002 AWP Award Series in Poetry, University of Pittsburgh Press, 2003 and *The Country of Women*, Calyx Books, 1995. Her poems have appeared over the past thirty-five years in journals including *Prairie Schooner, The New Republic*, and *Beloit Poetry Journal*.

Judy Kronenfeld's most recent books of poetry are *Shimmer* (WordTech Editions, 2012) and the second edition of *Light Lowering in Diminished Sevenths* (Antrim House, 2012), winner of the 2007 Litchfield Review Poetry Book Prize. Her poems have appeared in many print and online journals (such as *Calyx, Cimarron Review, Natural Bridge, Valparaiso Poetry Review, Sequestrum, The Pedestal),* and in eighteen anthologies. http://judykronenfeld. com.

Sara Emily Kuntz has a BA in English from the University of Pittsburgh and a MFA in Creative Writing from Carlow University. As an enterprising copy shop employee she self-published ten single poem mini-books, as well as a small run chapbook. She has been published in *Rivet, Stone Highway Review, Cabildo Quarterly, Rust + Moth*, and *Cactus Heart*. Sara lives in Brooklyn with a big grey cat named Miso, like the soup.

Michelle Robin La's first book, *Catching Shrimp with Bare Hands*, is the story of her husband growing up in the midst of the Vietnam War and his struggle under Communism. Her thoughts on the challenge of writing about another culture appeared in *Literary Mama's* "After Page One" series. She lives with her husband and three children in Santa Barbara, CA. www.michellerobinla.com.

Lori Lamothe is the author of a full-length poetry collection, Trace *Elements* (Aldrich Press), and several chapbooks, including *Diary in Irregular Ink* (ELJ Publications). Her poems have appeared or are forthcoming in *Blackbird, Blue Lyra Review, CALYX, Painted Bride Quarterly* and elsewhere. She lives in New England with her daughter and a red Siberian husky born on Halloween.

Poems by **Elizabeth Lara** have appeared in print and online, including in *Mom Egg Review; Edna, Issue 4; Confluencia in the Valley: The First Five Years of Converging with Words; unFold;* and *The Vine Leaves Literary Journal*. In 2011 she was a resident at the Millay Colony in Austerlitz, NY. She is a member of the Hot Poets Collective, whose anthology, *Of Fire, Of Iron*, was published in 2012. She lives in New York and Santo Domingo, Dominican Republic.

Anna Lawson is an artist living in a small ex-mining village in the North East of England. Based on her experiences as a working mother, a lecturer in Fine Art and Art History and an artist, her images communicate weighty, emotional but universal experiences of women. More info about Anna and featured art may be found on our website, www.momeggreview.com, in the Gallery.

Deborah Leipziger is an author, poet, and professor. Her chapbook, *Flower Map*, was published by Finishing Line Press (2013). In 2014, her poem "Written on Skin" was nominated for a Pushcart Prize. She is the co-founder of *Soul-Lit*, an on-line poetry magazine. http://soul-lit.com. Born in Brazil, Ms. Leipziger is the author of several books on human rights. To read her poetry, go to http://flowermap.net/.

Lori Levy's poems have been published in literary journals in the U.S., England, and Israel. She lives in Los Angeles with her husband, but "home" has also been Vermont and Israel at other times of her life. Her two little grandchildren keep her smiling and entertained.

Tsaurah Litzky is a Pushcart Prize nominated poet who also writes fiction, creative nonfiction, memoir, plays, erotica, and commentary. Poetry is her heart. Her recent poetry chapbook, *Jerry in the Bardo* (NightBallet Press) is in its third printing. She is also a collage artist and a Yoga teacher. Tsaurah loves *Mom Egg Review* because it is so important, vital, wonderful. Contact Tsaurah@mindspring.com.

Renee Beauregard Lute lives and writes in Issaquah, Washington with her husband and two children. Visit her at http://reneebeauregardlute.com.

Charlotte Mandel's ninth book of poetry, *Through a Garden Gate*, with color photographs by Vincent Covello, is newly published by David Robert Books. Previous titles include *Life Work, Rock Vein Sky*, and two poem-novellas of feminist biblical re-vision—*The Life of Mary* and *The Marriages of Jacob*. She is winner of the New Jersey Poets Prize. Visit her at charlottemandel.com.

Jennifer Martelli's chapbook, *Apostrophe*, was published by Big Table Publishing Company. Her work has appeared most recently in *Tar River Poetry, burntdistrict, Bop Dead City, *82, A Narrow Fellow*, and as a feature in *Right Hand Pointing*. Her work has been nominated for a Pushcart Prize and she is the recipient of the Massachusetts Cultural Council Grant in Poetry. She's taught high school English and women's literature at Emerson College. She is an associate editor for *The Compassion Project: An Anthology*, and lives in Marblehead, Massachusetts with her family. www.jennifermartelli.com.

Rethabile Masilo blogs at Poéfrika and co-edits *Canopic Jar*. He is a Mosotho poet who lives in Paris, France, with his wife and two children. His work has been published in various magazines. Rethabile was born in 1961 in Lesotho and left his country with his parents and siblings to go into exile in 1981. He moved through the Republic of South Africa (very short stay, on account of the weight of apartheid), Kenya and the United States of America, before settling in France in 1987. In 2012 his first book of poems, *Things That Are Silent*, was published by Pindrop Press.

Grace Mattern's poems and prose have appeared in *The Sun, Prairie Schooner, Hanging Loose, Calyx* and elsewhere. She has received fellowships from the NH State Arts Council and Vermont Studio Center and has published two books of poetry. She has worked in the movement to end violence against women for 35 years. She blogs at www.gracemattern.com.

Libby Maxey is part of the staff at the online journal *Literary Mama*, which has also published her poetry. She is a founding member of the acquisitions editorial board of Thornapple Books, a small press imprint for literary fiction. Further, she is the mother of two little boys.

Megan Merchant is forthcoming. Her chapbook, *Translucent, Sealed*, is forthcoming though Dancing Girl Press. Her first full-length collection, *Gravel Ghosts,* is forthcoming though Glass Lyre Press. Her first children's book, *These Words I've Shaped For You*, is forthcoming through Philomel Books. Her future is bright. She wears shades.

Colleen Michaels, host of *The Improbable Places Poetry Tour,* lives and works in Beverly, Massachusetts. Her poetry has appeared in journals and anthologies; installations of her poems have appeared on bar coasters, shower curtains, in the Peabody Essex Museum, and on the stairs to Crane Beach in Ipswich, Massachusetts.

Matt W. Miller is the author of *Club Icarus*, winner of the Vassar Miller Poetry Prize, and *Cameo Diner: Poems*. A former Wallace Stegner Fellow, he has published work in Southwest Review, Harvard Review, Slate, Florida Review, Briar Cliff Review and Profane, among other journals. He teaches English and coaches football at Phillips Exeter Academy.

John Minczeski is the author of several previous books of poetry, including *A Letter to Serafin* (University of Akron Press, 2009). His work has appeared in *Mid-American Review, Pleiades*, and others, including a previous issue of *Mom Egg Review*. He lives in St. Paul, and teaches poetry workshops around Minnesota.

Katrinka Moore's most recent book is *Numa* (Aqueduct Press, 2014). She is the author of *Thief* (BlazeVOX, 2009), and *This is Not a Story* (Finishing Line Press, 2003), which won the New Women's Voices Prize.

Elizabeth Deanna Morris Lakes has a BA in Creative Writing from Susquehanna University. She is currently pursuing her MFA at George Mason University. She has appeared in *{Ex}tinguished & {Ex}tinct: An Anthology of Things That No Longer {Ex}ist, Whiskey Island, OVS*, and *Hot Metal Bridge*. She has a chapbook, *Patterning*, from Corgi Snorkel Press.

Wendy Jones Nakanishi, an American by birth, has been resident in Japan for thirty years. She publishes academic articles on 18th, 19th, 20th and 21st-century English and Japanese literature and creative non-fiction pieces about her life in Japan as a university professor, the wife a Japanese farmer, and the mother of three sons.

Amy Scanlan O'Hearn teaches literature and creative writing in New Jersey and is a graduate of the MFA program at Rutgers University. Her fiction is published in *The Bacopa Literary Review*, she is the recipient of the New Poetry Award by the Oregon Poet's Association and is happy to have her work appear in *Mom Egg Review*.

January Gill O'Neil is the author of *Misery Islands* (fall 2014) and *Underlife* (2009), both published by CavanKerry Press. She is the executive director of the Massachusetts Poetry Festival and an assistant professor of English at Salem State University.

Eve Packer is a Bronx-born, poet/performer/actress. Three books from *Fly By Night* press, the most recent, *new nails*. Five poetry/jazz CD's, four w/ saxophonist Noah Howard, and one w/pianist/vocalist Stephanie Stone & others. Lives downtown, swims daily, mom, grandmom, happy to be part of *Mom Egg Review*.

Dawn Paul teaches writing at Montserrat College of Art. She is the author of two novels, *The Country of Loneliness* and *Still River*. Her poetry has been published most recently in the *Naugatuck River Review* and the *Lindenwood Review*. She is also a frequent performer on the Improbable Places Poetry Tour.

Puma Perl is a performer, producer, and a widely published poet/writer. She is the author of two chapbooks, *Belinda and Her Friends* and *Ruby True*, and two full-length collections, *knuckle tattoos* and *Retrograde*. As Puma Perl and Friends, she performs with some of NYC's best musicians and merges poetry with rock n roll. More information, including links to her videos can be found on her blog: http://pumaperl.blogspot.com/.

Virginia Petrucci is a freelance writer and artist. Her work has appeared/will appear in *Another Chicago Magazine, Hermeneutic Chaos Literary Journal, Dirty Chai, Snow Monkey, AITIA: Philosophy-Humanities,* and *Best New Writing* 2014 as runner up for the Gover Prize in Flash Fiction. She has written for the *LA Post-Examiner*. She lives in Los Angeles with her son.

Deborah Polikoff grew up to the sound of her mother's typewriter. Winner of the 1977 Radcliffe Poetry Prize, she has published poetry in *The Madison Review, Radcliffe Quarterly, Annapurna, Touch,* and been anthologized in *Clarify* and *The Poet's Guide to New Hampshire*. She is a consultant for the *A Room of Her Own (AROHO)* 2015 retreat, Ghost Ranch, New Mexico. www.deborahpolikoff.com.

Andrea Potos is the author of five poetry collections, including *New Girl* (Anchor & Plume Press), *We Lit The Lamps Ourselves* (Salmon Poetry) and *Yaya's Cloth* (Iris Press). Another collection from Salmon Poetry entitled *An Ink Like Early Twilight* will be published in 2015. Her work appears widely in print and online.

Kyle Potvin's first collection of poetry, *Sound Travels on Water* (Finishing Line Press) was co-winner of the New England Poetry Club's 2014 Jean Pedrick Chapbook Award. She was named a finalist for the 2008 Howard Nemerov Sonnet Award. Her poetry has appeared in *The New York Times, Measure, The Huffington Post, JAMA,* among others. www.KylePotvin.com

Margaret (Peg) Rapp is a feminist, writer, mother and political activist. Her one act plays "The Game" and "Dorothy and the Wiseman of Ooze " have been produced out West. Ms. Rapp is currently living in New York where she writes short stories and participates in blogs at http://www.dailykos.com/user/geminijen. She is also working on a political novel satirizing the New Left.

Francine Rockey is a poet, children's author, and freelance writer. She studied literature at Arizona State University and completed her graduate degree at San Diego State University. Her work was recently in the *SDPA* and the *Journal of Adolescent Adult Literacy*. She lives with her husband and son in San Diego, CA. Her favorite word is giggle.

Wesley Rothman's poems and criticism have appeared in *32 Poems, Crab Orchard Review, New England Review, PANK, Post Road, Prairie Schooner, Rattle, Vinyl,* and *The White Review*, among other venues. Recipient of a Vermont Studio Center fellowship as well as Puschart Prize and Best of the Net nominations, he teaches writing and cultural literatures throughout Boston. http://wesleyrothman.wordpress.com/.

Margaret Rozga has published three books: *Justice   Freedom   Herbs, Though I Haven't Been to Baghdad ,* and *200 Nights and One Day .* Her Pushcart Prize nominated essay "Community Inclusive: A Poetics to Move Us Forward" is included in the anthology *Local Grounds*. She has been a resident at Ragdale and a Creative Fellow at the American Antiquarian Society.

Sarah Sadie blogs about theology and poetry at patheos.com. Her poetry has received the Council for Wisconsin Writers' Niedecker and Posner Prizes, and a Pushcart Prize. One of two Poets Laureate of Madison, Wisconsin, her collection, *Somewhere Piano,* was published in 2012 by Mayapple Press. She teaches at the University of Iowa Summer Writing Festival, and sometimes elsewhere.

Wendy Scott's first book, *Soon I Will Build an Ark,* was published by Main Street Rag in 2014. Her work has appeared in *Harpur Palate, Paterson Literary Review, The Meadow,* and others. She has an MFA from the University of Pittsburgh, two grown (amazing) sons, and lives in Pittsburgh.

Margie Shaheed is a community poet, writer and teaching artist. Her poems from *The Playground* are the winner of the 2014 Hidden Charm Press Chapbook contest and will be published in June 2015. Her other available poetry chapbooks are *Mosaic* (2013) and *Onomatopoeia* (2015) both published by NightBallet Press. You can find her stories from *The Playground* published at www.TimBookTu.com.

Sarah Shamel has been writing poetry and short prose since her third child was born in 2012. She lives, and was raised, in Massachusetts where she has always enjoyed the open space of historic New England cemeteries. Sarah facilitates semi-annual Mothers' Open Mics, north of Boston. This is her first publication. https://www.facebook.com/groups/538779649514877/.

Lynne Shapiro is a poet living in Hoboken, New Jersey. Her poems have been published in *Mom Egg Review* and other print and on-line magazines, as well as in anthologies about mushrooms, clothing, and pain and healing.

Ana C. H. Silva lives in Spanish Harlem, NYC with her husband and 7 year old twin daughters. Her poetry has been published in *Podium, Mom Egg Review, the nth position, Snow Monkey, Anemone Sidecar,* and *StepAway Magazine.* She won the 2010 inaugural Rachel Wetzsteon Memorial Poetry Prize at the 92ndSt. Y Unterberg Poetry Center.

Judith Skillman is the author of fifteen books of poetry. Her work has appeared in *Tampa Review, Cimarron Review, Tar River Poetry, Prairie Schooner, FIELD, Seneca Review, The Iowa Review, Southern Review, Poetry, New Poets of the American West,* and other journals and anthologies. Visit www.judithskillman.com.

Darcy Smith's poems have been published in various literary journals including *Boyne Berries* based in Ireland. Other publications include *Up The River* and *Chronogram,* both based in the Hudson River Valley of New York State where she works and writes.

Meghan Smith teaches English at Lawrence Academy in Groton, Massachusetts where she lives with her husband and daughter. Between paper grading and playground trips, she writes short fiction and poetry.

Rose M. Smith's work has appeared in *The Pedestal Magazine, The Examined Life, Pavement Saw, Main Street Rag, Boston Literary Magazine, Kinfolks Quarterly* and others. She is author of three chapbooks and was co-editor of *Cap City Poets: Columbus and Central Ohio's Best Known, Read, and Requested Poets* (Pudding House Publications, 2008). Rose is a Cave Canem Fellow.

Emily Spencer is a graduate student, studying the Master of Education at The Ohio State University. Her work has been published in **82 Review* and *BLACKBERRY: a magazine.* http://emilyspencer.net.

Autumn Stephens is the author of the *Wild Women* series of women's history and humor, editor of two personal essay anthologies, and former co-editor of The East Bay Monthly. She has written for *The New York Times, The San Francisco Chronicle,* and numerous other publications. She conducts writing workshops for cancer survivors in Oakland, Calif., and teaches private writing classes.

Alison Stone wrote *Dangerous Enough, Borrowed Logic, From the Fool to the World,* and *They Sing at Midnight,* which won the 2003 Many Mountains Moving Award. She was awarded Poetry's Frederick Bock Prize and New York Quarterly's Madeline Sadin award. She created The Stone Tarot and is a licensed psychotherapist. www.stonepoetry.org www.stonetarot.com.

Enzo Silon Surin is a Haitian-born poet, publisher, social advocate and the author of *Higher Ground* (Finishing Line Press). His poetry is forthcoming and has appeared in *The BreakBeat Poets* anthology, *Ozone Park Journal, sx salon, Tidal Basin Review, The Caribbean Writer,* among others. He holds an MFA in Creative Writing and serves as Assistant Professor of English at Bunker Hill Community College. www.enzosurinink.org.

Marjorie Thomsen's poems have been published in *Haibun Today, Literary Mama, Poetica Magazine* and elsewhere. She won the New England Poetry Club's 2012 Firman Houghton Award. Her first book of poetry, *Pretty Things Please* will be published next year by WordTechCommunications/Turning Point. She was raised in Richmond, Virginia and now lives in Cambridge, Massachusetts with her husband and three children.

Meredith Trede's book, *Field Theory*, was published by SFA Press. A Toadlily Press founder, her chapbook, *Out of the Book*, was in the inaugural Quartet Series. Other journal publications include *Barrow Street, Blue Mesa Review*, and *The Paris Review*. She has been awarded residency fellowships at Blue Mountain Center, Ragdale, Saltonstall, VCCA, and the Nicholson Political Poetry Award. www.meredithtrede.com.

Claudia Van Gerven's work has been published in a number of journals including *Prairie Schooner, Georgetown Review,* and *Calyx.* Her work has appeared in numerous anthologies and has been nominated for the Pushcart Prize. Her four chapbooks include *The Ends of Sunbonnet Sue,* (winner of the Angel Fish Prize), *Amazing Grace* and *Totem* (Green Fuse Press), and *Bearing Witness* (Finishing Line Press).

Susan Vespoli lives in Phoenix with her 3-legged dog, Jack. She is a teacher, poet, and born-again-bicyclist. Susan received her MFA from Antioch University L.A. and has had poems and essays published in various online and print journals.

The poems of **Lisa Vihos** have appeared in *Big Muddy, Camel Saloon, Forge, Main Street Rag, Seems, Verse Wisconsin,* and other journals. She has two chapbooks, *A Brief History of Mail* and *The Accidental Present* and two Pushcart nominations. She is the poetry and arts editor for *Stoneboat* and an occasional guest blogger for Best American Poetry online. Visit her own blog at Frying the Onion.

Nancy Vona worked as an editor and teacher for many years. The birth of her first child renewed her love of creative writing. Her poems and creative non-fiction have been published in several remarkable literary journals, including *Spillway, Mom Egg Review,* and *Naugatuck River Review.* She is grateful to the editors of these publications for keeping poetry alive and honoring the magic of creative writing.

Anna Lowe Weber, originally from Louisiana, currently lives in Huntsville, Alabama where she teaches creative writing at the University of Alabama in Huntsville. Recent work has appeared or is forthcoming in *Rattle, Bluestem,* and *Reunion: The Dallas Review,* among other journals.

Laura Grace Weldon is the author of a recent poetry collection, Tending, and a handbook of alternative education, Free Range Learning. She's written poetry with nursing home residents, used poetry to teach nonviolence, and painted poems on beehives although her work appears in more conventional places such as *Christian Science Monitor, J Journal, Literary Mama, Shot Glass Journal,* and *Pudding House.* lauragraceweldon. com.

Shanna Powlus Wheeler directs the Writing Center at Lycoming College and teaches first-year writing courses. Her poetry chapbook, *Lo & Behold*, was published by Finishing Line Press. Her individual poems have appeared in a wide range of journals, such as *Crab Orchard Review* and *Mezzo Cammin*. She lives with her husband and daughter near Williamsport, Pennsylvania. Visit her site at www.shannapowluswheeler.wordpress.com.

Artress Bethany White earned an M.A. in creative writing from New York University, and a Ph.D. in English from the University of Kentucky. Her poetry has recently appeared in *Harvard Review, Mud Season Review,* and *Black Renaissance Noire* and is forthcoming in *The New Guard. Fast Fat Girls in Pink Hot Pants* (Aldabra Press, 2012) is her first collection of poetry.

Quinn White is the author of *My Moustache* (Dancing Girl Press, 2013) and *Orienteering* (Origami Poems Project, 2013).

Lisa Wiley is an English professor at Erie Community College in Buffalo, NY where she co-hosts the Just Buffalo Literary Café. She is the author of *Chamber Music*, a chapbook of 21 villanelles (Finishing Line Press, 2013). Her poetry has appeared in *Earth's Daughters, Epiphany Magazine, The Healing Muse, Medical Journal of Australia, Rockhurst Review*, and *Yale Journal for Humanities in Medicine*. Contact: wileymoz@yahoo.com.

Faith Williams has been exchanging poems with a friend for a long time, since 1977. She published early on while teaching and then stopped while a librarian. Her poems have appeared in a number of journals, including *Calyx, Sow's Ear, Poet Lore*, and *Nimrod*.

L.B. Williams is the author of, *Letters to Virginia Woolf*, (Hamilton Books, 2005). Her poetry has appeared in such publications as *Washington Square, Mom Egg Review, Sunrise from Blue Thunder* (A Pirene's Fountain Anthology). She has also published two poetry chapbooks, *Sky Studies,* (Finishing Line Press Fall 2014), and *The Eighth Phrase* (Porkbelly Press, October 2014). She is Professor of Literature at Ramapo College of New Jersey. www.letterstovirginiawoolf.com.

Nancy Lynée Woo is a 2015 PEN Center USA Emerging Voices Fellow, and co-founder and editor of a socially conscious literary press called *Lucid Moose Lit*. She is currently working on a collection of poems about her mixed heritage, called *The Great Divide*. Often caught cavorting around Long Beach, CA, this poet can also be found at nancylyneewoo.com.

Müesser Yeniay has won several prizes in Turkey. Her books are *Dibine Düşüyor Karanlık da* (2009), *Evimi Dağlara Kurdum* (translation), *Yeniden Çizdim Göğü* (2011), *The Other Consciousness: Surrealism* and *The Second New* (2013), *Before Me There Were Deserts* (2014); also *Contemporary Spanish Anthology* with Metin Cengiz and Jaime B. Rosa. Her poems have been translated into various languages. Müesser is the editor of the literature magazine *Şiirden* (of Poetry). She is currently pursuing a PhD in Turkish literature at Bilkent University, Ankara, and is also a member of PEN and the Writers Syndicate of Turkey.

MOM EGG REVIEW

Mom Egg Review Issues Available

Vol. 13 "Compassionate Action" 2015 Paper, 154 pp. $18
Vol. 12   2014 Paper, 150 pp. $18
Vol. 11 "Mother Tongue"   2013 Paper, 125 pp. $18
Vol. 10 "The Body"   2012 Paper, 120 pp. $18
Vol. 9   2011 Paper, 120 pp. $18
Vol. 8 "Lessons"   2010 Paper, 120 pp. $18
Vol. 7   2009 Paper, 124 pp. $18
Vol. 6   2008 Paper, 114 pp. $18
Vol. 5   2007 Paper, 101 pp. $18

*Plus US shipping $3.50 for the first book, $1.00 for each additional book.

Email info@themomegg.com for info about discounts for quantity purchases and for classroom use, or for out-of-country shipping.

Subscribe to MER

Shipping is free for subscription copies!

One year $18
Two years $36

Mail your order with a check to

Mom Egg Review
Half-Shell Press
PO Box 9037
Bardonia, NY 10954

MOM EGG REVIEW
Literature & Art

Contact: info@themomegg.com

Order on the web at
www.momeggreview.com (Click "Shop")